Preparation
for Ministry

Preparation
for Ministry

Allan Harman

THE BANNER OF TRUTH TRUST

THE BANNER OF TRUTH TRUST
3 Murrayfield Road, Edinburgh EH12 6EL, UK
P.O. Box 621, Carlisle, PA 17013, USA

*

© Allan Harman 2015

ISBN:
Print: 978-1-84871-623-0
EPUB: 978-1-84871-624-7
Kindle: 978-1-84871-626-1

*

Typeset in 10/15 pt Sabon Oldstyle Figures at the
Banner of Truth Trust, Edinburgh
Printed in the USA by
Versa Press, Inc.,
East Peoria, IL

CONTENTS

Introduction   vii

1. Coming to Faith   1

2. The Call to the Ministry   3

3. Pre-Theologial Study   13

4. Choosing a Theological College or Seminary   19

5. The Theological Course   23

6. Early Ministry   27

7. Staying Fresh   37

    Conclusion   43

    Short Bibliography   45

    Appendix 1: Suggested Preparatory Reading   49

    *Appendix 2: A Short Guide to Sermon
       Preparation*   53

    Appendix 3: The Minister's Self-Watch   59

    *Appendix 4: The Religious Life of
       Theological Students*   93

INTRODUCTION

THIS little book deals with questions relating to a call to ministry, theological training, and entry into pastoral work. It comes out of my own experiences as student, pastor, and seminary teacher. I came from a pastor's family, so I had the advantage of seeing my father carrying out ministry. We often had other pastors or missionaries staying in our home, and, especially after my conversion as a teenager, I learned much from conversations with them. Later, I was helped in many pastoral situations by knowing how my father had acted in similar ones in his ministry.

My aim, when I sensed God's call to service in the ministry, was to be a pastor of a local church. That has always remained my aim, even though I have spent many years teaching in colleges and seminaries. I have never made the disjunction between pastor and scholar, as throughout my teaching career I have been active both in the local and wider church, engaging in preaching and pastoral work. I have tried to give practical advice that may help those who are contemplating studying for the ministry, or those already in training, or early in the ministry.

1

Coming to Faith

BEFORE dealing with questions relating to a call to the ministry, theological courses, and settling into a congregation as pastor, matters relating to our standing with God have to be faced. You need to know that you are right with God if you are going to call others into obedience to Christ.

a. *According to the New Testament, calling to the ministry is a work of God.* Hence, making decisions regarding it is not just a matter of the human mind working out all the positives and negatives about it. While the mind has to be involved, it must be informed by the operation of God's Holy Spirit. Divine work requires a divine calling.

b. *There is no place in ministry for an unconverted pastor.* No one who is unsure about his relationship with God should consider the Christian ministry. It is a divinely ordained task of proclaiming the gospel of God's grace in Christ. It is a task for those who have come to faith in the Lord Jesus and who know the regenerating power of the Holy Spirit. To enter the ministry without a work of God in the heart and life is completely alien to the New Testament. Serving in ministry will not lead to your own conversion. It requires prior experience of God's grace in Christ.

c. Self-examination is a biblical directive. You need to examine yourself whether you are in the faith (2 Cor. 13:5). This biblical injunction must be heeded. It is not for others to tell you that you are converted; you have to tell them. It is not without reason that Scottish Presbyterian churches often, in the past, prescribed William Guthrie's book, *The Christian's Great Interest,* for student reading early in the course of study.[1]

[1] William Guthrie, *The Christian's Great Interest* (Edinburgh: Banner of Truth Trust, 1982).

2

The Call to the Ministry

THE Christian ministry is a great work. Warren and David Wiersbe say concerning it: 'be encouraged— the ministry is a great calling, and with God's help, you will make it'.[1] But to take encouragement, you need to know what exactly is involved in ministry and how you become convinced that the ministry is God's plan for your life.

The New Testament does not have a definition of 'ministry'. Instead it gives us examples of ministry, and instructions that help us focus on its major aspects. Preaching and teaching are clearly central—'preach the word'—for that is the communication of God's truth to men by men with the express purpose of producing behavioural change. In other words, presentation of the

[1] Warren W. Wiersbe and David W. Wiersbe, *Making Sense of the Ministry: How to Apply Your Education to the Pastorate* (Grand Rapids: Baker Book House, 1983), p. 28.

gospel has as its first aim the conversion of listeners, and then helping them grow as Christians and become mature in Christ. In the early church deacons were appointed so that the apostles could give themselves to the ministry of the word and prayer (Acts 6:3-4).

The Bible gives us illustrations of men called by God to be his messengers, but many of these are extraordinary, such as Isaiah's vision of the exalted Lord (Isa. 6:1-13), or Amos' call from farming pursuits to preach in the northern kingdom of Israel (Amos 7:10-16), or Paul's vision of the Lord on the road to Damascus (Acts 9:3-9). No instruction is given that you must have similar experiences before you can claim to have a call to the ministry, nor should we think that God usually calls in these dramatic ways. The epistles of the New Testament, especially the so-called pastoral epistles of Paul (1 and 2 Timothy, and Titus), provide the basic instructions for Christian ministry. They are part of the teaching books of the New Testament, that contain the material brought to the remembrance of the apostles by the work of the Holy Spirit (John 14:26). Patterns of ministry are set out there for the church to follow.

a. How does God call? Though some receive a call to the ministry in dramatic fashion, for most it occurs over a period of time. Often there is development in understanding of what the ministry is, and also what constitutes a call to it. It may be part of your maturing in the faith, as you grow as a Christian and understand more of God's claims upon you. As Christians we confess that we have been bought with a price (1 Cor. 6:19-20). However, the full realisation of Christ's lordship over you may not be experienced until some time has passed in the walk of faith. That lordship is intrusive, and you should be prepared for service opportunities that may surprise you, and calling into the ministry may well be one of those surprises. While some pattern often emerges when you reflect with others on your call, yet your calling is individual to yourself as God works out his will in your life.[2]

b. Assessing your own call. This is the personal aspect of the call, and it should involve two factors. First, the consciousness that God is indeed calling you into ministry. There must be the overriding awareness that there is no other course of action for you to take. God must so work in your life that you feel constrained to give yourself to one vocation alone, the work of ministry in Christ's church. The love of Christ must hem you in

[2] There is a very helpful discussion by Joel Nederhood, 'The Minister's Call' in Samuel T. Logan, Jr., *The Preacher and Preaching: Reviving the Art in the Twentieth Century* (Phillipsburg, NJ: Presbyterian and Reformed Publishing Company, 2011), pp. 33-61.

to this particular course of action (2 Cor. 5:14-15, 20). Second, the personal assessment of whether you have the necessary qualifications to ministry. This includes asking yourself various questions such as these:

- Am I passionate about the Bible as God's word?

- Do I have a single-minded commitment about the proclamation of Christ to the lost?

- Am I compelled towards Christian ministry?

- Have I the intellectual capacity to cope both with study and also years in the ministry?

- Have I shown the capacity for speaking in public?

- Do I relate easily to people of a variety of ages and backgrounds?

- Do I work easily with others?

- Have I also shown leadership skills?

c. The call to ministry has also to be tested objectively. This means that outside of your own feelings and convictions there has to be testing of the call. This is necessary, for ministry is not an activity in which you are to engage in isolation from the wider Christian community. It is an activity of the church and hence gifts must be tested. Some of the questions you have to ask yourself, others in the church must also ask of you. Your sense of call must be confirmed by the local church.[3] Pastor and office bearers in the local congregation need to be approached, first informally and then perhaps in a formal setting. The church leadership must be convinced by observation of your life and service that you have the heart for ministry and have already exhibited the gifts for such ministry. If anyone says to me they have a call to the ministry, but I know they have never done anything in their local church, I suggest they should go and consult their local church leaders. If they claim to have the gifts of ministry, why has their home church not seen these and offered ministry opportunities? Has the leadership failed to be perceptive in judging suitability for full-time Christian service, or is it the case that they have come to the view that ministry gifts are not present in the aspiring candidate?

Various schemes have been put in place for apprenticeships in ministry to enable students to work in the setting of a local congregation, and so gauge their capacity for ministerial training. Nothing is wrong with this idea, but it should not be assumed that this is the only way to progress to full-time study. In fact, some enter ministry apprenticeships while they are still imma-

[3] For a discussion on this, see Brian Croft, *Test, train, affirm and send into ministry: Recovering the local church's responsibility in the external call* (Leominster: Day One, 2010).

ture in the faith, and they do not have the theological knowledge that is a necessary prerequisite. Just as there are many ways to come to faith in Christ, so there are many ways that God may use to bring you to the point of formally entering a course of theological training.

The capacity to cope with intense study, not just during a theological course but in ministry itself, is also important. Ministry requires much reading and study, and if that is going to be a problem, it should be recognised as early as possible. A call to ministry later in life, for example, can be intellectually challenging. Enrolling in a single subject, or doing an evening course, is a good way of testing the ability to cope with a full-time course. There are many theological courses available on the internet, though many from colleges and seminaries that are for credit can be expensive.[4]

Two other points need to be made. With individualism rampant, it is often the case that someone will enter theological study and then proceed to some form of ministry without consulting others in the church.

[4] The Reformed Theological College, Geelong, Australia, has a free course entitled 'Introduction to Theology'. It can be accessed at www.rtc.org.au. Third Millennium ministries (CEO Dr Richard Pratt) has developed a range of very good courses, available in several languages, for which no fees are charged (http:thirdmill.org). If prospective students wish to gain a deeper understanding of theology, they can download lecture series from Reformed Theological Seminary (www.rts.edu). This does not involve registering and paying for courses for credit.

They feel that they owe no responsibility to others in the body of Christ. Fitness for study and ministry in these cases is self-assessed.

On the other hand, some prospective students come from a church or a church body that has not had many recent applicants. The joy in having another candidate can sometimes be so great that the warning signs are overlooked. I can recall several cases of this nature. One student took my advice after a year of study to suspend his candidature, returned to his former profession, and served admirably in the local church. Some others refused to accept the advice, and completed their theological course. However, either they did not receive a call to a congregation, or in their first pastorate the lack of ministerial gifts became very evident and they demitted, never returning to ministry. The ability to complete a theological course is not the sole criterion for ministry. There must be the appropriate character qualifications and gifts for the varied tasks a minister has to perform.

d. Seeking the judgment and advice of others. A true estimate of your own gifts does not come from self-assessment. You need to submit yourself to others so that your gifts can be tested. In many cases it is the pastor or the elders in the local congregation who can judge best whether an applicant has given appropriate indications of ministerial ability. Various matters need addressing:

- Evidence of a true conversion experience.

- On-going evidence of spiritual life and growth in grace.

- Demonstration in the local church of talents needed in ministry: including a servant mentality, gifts displayed in teaching children and adults, ability to speak on Scripture, an evident love of people and care for them.

- Aptitude for reading and study.

e. The need to assess your family situation, especially your wife's attitude. Anyone thinking of theological study with a view to the ministry or missionary service must be realistic in regard to the family. If you are married, your wife must share the same spiritual experience as you, and heartily acquiesce in your sense of call to the ministry. For married couples, ministry is a team effort, and while history can show some cases where a ministry is blessed in spite of a wife's lack of spirituality, the norm is for complete unanimity between husband and wife in serving the Lord.

Other considerations must also be weighed. If you decide after some period in a work situation to study for the ministry, your wife's attitude is very important. She married you when you were an engineer, or architect, or whatever, while now you are suggesting a radical change of direction that will have important ramifications for her and your whole family. The decision to prepare for the ministry may involve a big change in the financial status of your family, several years of intense study by you, and at the end of it a totally new relationship for the wife of the 'new pastor'.[5]

The changes involving family should be canvassed thoroughly lest misapprehensions mar your marriage and detract from study and future ministry. Some conversations with other students or ministry couples may allay any doubts and help to prepare for the new situations and tasks ahead. The more discussion and acceptance of advice prior to entering into study for the ministry, the more fruitful that time will be. You can profit from the experiences of others, and hopefully avoid some of the pitfalls they have met with.

[5] For discussion on the privileges and problems of being a pastor's wife, see Ann Benton and friends, *The Minister's Wife: Privileges, Pressures and Pitfalls* (Nottingham: Inter-Varsity, 2011).

3

Pre-Theological Study

IF you have come to the point of knowing that you are going to prepare for the ministry, then you should try and make the most of your time before you actually begin your theological studies.

a. Give attention to your own growth as a Christian. Personal spiritual life and growth is crucial. There has to be discipline in your Bible study, attendance at fellowship groups, and regular worship on the Lord's day. Consecutive Bible reading is essential. This was once taken for granted, but now there is a need to encourage prospective students to make sure they are thoroughly familiar with the text of the English Bible. Adopt some scheme so that you cover all the Bible at least every year.[1] Whatever version of the Bible you use (providing

[1] Geoffrey Thomas, *Reading the Bible* (Edinburgh: Banner of Truth Trust, 1981) includes a Bible reading scheme, as does Sinclair B. Ferguson's *From the Mouth of God: Trusting, Reading, and Applying*

it is not a paraphrase such as the *New Living Bible* or *The Message*), continue to use it exclusively for your own reading. You must become very familiar with it and constant reading will help to cement the words into your memory. Other Bible versions are for the shelf, to be consulted when the need arises, for example, when wrestling with a difficult passage.

b. Start to read as widely as possible, not only in newer literature but in older books too. Ask advice from mature Christians regarding a suitable reading programme. The plethora of Christian literature presently available is in marked contrast to many of the periods in the past. This is a blessing on the one hand, but it also creates a danger on the other. It is a blessing that good books, written from solid biblical convictions, are readily available at attractive prices. However, don't imagine that all the books you find in a Christian bookshop are suitable, or are going to help you in your growth in Christian knowledge. Many books on sale today, despite their attractiveness, will not build up

---

the Bible (Edinburgh: Banner of Truth, 2014). Copies of Robert Murray M'Cheyne's scheme for daily Bible reading can be ordered from the Trust's website. It is also found in Andrew Bonar, *Memoir and Remains of Robert Murray M'Cheyne* (Edinburgh: Banner of Truth, 1973), pp. 618-28. A Bible reading scheme by Benjamin Shaw, Greenville Presbyterian Theological Seminary, is available to download at www.gpts.edu/resources/documents/oneyrbible.pdf.

in the faith. Discernment regarding the strengths and weaknesses of particular books is necessary, and such discernment may not come to the student until a little later. That is why the advice of trusted friends is absolutely essential at this early stage.[2]

c. Build resources for ministry including starting your own library. Any prospective student has probably already begun to gather books after his conversion, but the process must undoubtedly continue. Some books will be purchased on the recommendation of Christian friends. Others will be discovered by browsing in Christian bookshops or on the web. It is better to have fewer books that are well read rather than a large library of unread books. Some general one-volumed commentaries are a must in any library, as are good reference books such as Bible dictionaries. Biographies of Christians are important, as you can learn much about Christian discipleship and ministry from them. Be discerning when buying books during your course of studies. Some books you have to read may be important for a particular course of study but will not be very useful in later ministry. Try and assess what the value of a book is for the work of the ministry.

[2] See Appendix 1 for some suggested preliminary reading in different areas of theology.

d. Develop skills that will make the theological course easier. So many students are now using computers, yet many are not touch-typing. A couple of hours a day for several weeks can enable you to touch-type, and this in turn speeds up the process of getting information onto the computer. Likewise some reading on language acquisition will assist you in grasping the linguistic concepts that you will face when tackling Hebrew and Greek. As many students find, learning the biblical languages forces you to think about your own language, and hence the study of English grammar will never go amiss. It will also ease the pressures of course work if you make a start with the biblical languages. Talk with your pastor and see if he will help, or if he will refer you to someone else who can.

e. In view of the role of the pastor in teaching, you should not only listen to good preaching but also consider examples from the past. You may learn much from reading the sermons of past eras, but remember that every generation is different, and therefore there may be elements in older sermons that would not be appropriate today. One sometimes hears expressions in contemporary sermons that immediately stand out as coming from a former age. That is to be expected if it is part of a direct quotation, but it is not appropriate if it has been borrowed and incorporated as part of the preacher's own speech. Learn from others, but do not imitate.

Some models from the past are more useful than others. In particular, Bishop J. C. Ryle (1816–1900) wrote in such simple English that his sermons and biblical expositions are good models to follow. His expositions of the Gospels are readily available, new and second-hand.[3] These expositions also break up the Gospel passages so helpfully that those beginning to preach will learn much about how to isolate sections of the text suitable for a sermon.

At this stage take opportunities to speak in public or to preach if these are offered to you. On the whole, don't try to preach from obviously difficult passages. Choose, rather, Scripture passages that have a straightforward message that you can break down into several main ideas.[4]

f. Assess accurately the financial needs for several years of full-time study. Theological study can be made very difficult if financial pressures continually intrude. I have seen students struggling to cope with study

---

[3] J. C. Ryle, *Expository Thoughts on the Gospels*, 7 vols. (Edinburgh: Banner of Truth, 2012).

[4] See Appendix 2 for some brief suggestions on how to approach the task of preparing a sermon.

because they have to work long hours in paid employment to continue to support themselves financially. I remember well one student who worked in a gas station from midnight to 8 a.m., and then had to be in class at 9 a.m. Progressively as the semester went on, he was finding it harder and harder to stay awake in classes and to complete the necessary assignments. It would be better to wait a year or two before entering theological training so that you can save up the required amount of money than entering precipitously without adequate resources guaranteed. Some will claim that if called, a student has to go forward in faith, but remember, the borderline between faith and folly can be very narrow!

4

Choosing a Theological College or Seminary

WHILE in the past a large number of ministerial candidates were sometimes trained by one pastor, this is not the norm now. The main reasons are that it is better to have a college/seminary with the necessary library facilities, and teachers who are skilled in particular disciplines, rather than depending on one man, with limited library resources, and whose time is restricted for teaching because of congregational commitments. It also means that students are interacting with other students, learning from them, and finding that their lives are being shaped by the community of faith that they have joined.

a. A right choice is essential. Care must be taken in the choice of where to study for ministry. A theological course is a deeply influential part of one's life. You are going to listen day after day to certain lecturers. You are going to interact with students from widely different backgrounds, perhaps very different from your own. All this means that you will be moulded by your theological course whether you are conscious of that or not.

b. Find out as much as you can about the seminaries you are considering. Read literature about them, visit them if possible, ask staff about their emphases and aims, and talk with graduates from them. You must gather as much information about each seminary you are considering in order to make an informed choice. Not all graduates from a particular institution will reflect its ethos, but many will display in their ministries the skills they learned there.

c. Specifically ask about the doctrinal stance of the seminary to which you attracted. You should not have to spend several years in fighting doctrinal wars as a student. It is often very hard for a young student to challenge a lecturer, and there is often a sense of having to conform with the teaching being received. Having said that, don't underestimate the changes that do come to one's thinking during a course.

d. Pick a seminary that has lecturers with pastoral experience. This should be a prerequisite, as those teaching should be directing their class teaching towards the work of the pastorate. The teaching should have a focus that is ministry orientated. My own pattern in teaching has been often to stop and say to students: 'How can we use this biblical teaching in our preaching?' I want them to know that I am not teaching esoteric material that, however relevant for academia, is irrelevant for people in the pew.

e. Candidates within a specific denomination may face hard decisions. That is because in many denominations it is demanded that students attend the theological education provided by the denomination. That system can work well if the candidate knows that his own convictions are the same as the denomination, and hence can attend a specific seminary institution knowing that the teaching accords with the denomination's doctrinal standard. If that is not so, a critical decision has to be made. Many students of conservative theological convictions have gone to a liberal denominational college only to have their faith undermined by the teaching and their vision of ministry completely altered. In some cases students can train in a non-denominational seminary but then gain access to ministry in their own denomination, though they may have to comply with requirements for some further study. In the main, I think intending students of a denominational college or seminary should assess whether their future lies in that denomination or not. If not, they should go to some other institution for their training.

5

The Theological Course

A course of study for the Christian ministry should be a blessing. It is a time of intense preoccupation with the Bible, Christian theology, and church history, together with training in many practical disciplines that are going to be part of your life in ministry.

a. Start out with the expectation that you are going to enjoy it and also grow as a Christian during the course. In theological teaching I normally begin a new course by saying to the students that the most important thing is not what grades they are going to get. Rather, the enjoyment of studying God's word together has to be foremost, and afterwards we must be able to think about the blessing that such study has brought.

b. Realise from the outset that study is hard work. The theological course is taxing, as is any serious course of study. It demands your time and energies, and will often be tiring. Some years ago, Prof. John Murray wrote about how, at times, biblical study may be heavy and even seem as dry as dust. But remember, he cautioned, dust has its place when you are dealing with gold dust![1]

c. Never separate off intellectual study and devotional. Sometimes it is suggested that there is a sharp distinction between our reading of Scripture and other literature for devotional use compared with our academic study of the same material. This distinction is false, because you have to approach Scripture with reverence whatever the particular reason for reading it. You can't compartmentalise your biblical study so that you can deal any more abstractly with it when it is for a different purpose. Scholar/pastor and pastor/scholar fit neatly together.[2]

From my own experience I can testify to times when I received great blessing, not when hearing a sermon, but when I was listening to an academic lecture on a passage of Scripture or on a theological topic. The truth

[1] John Murray, 'Systematic Theology' in Iain H. Murray, ed., *Collected Writings of John Murray, vol. 4 Studies in Theology*, p. 16 (Edinburgh: Banner of Truth, 1982), p. 16.

[2] See helpful discussion on this matter, with autobiographical material, by John Piper and Don Carson, *The Pastor as Scholar and the Scholar as Pastor* (Wheaton: Crossway, 2011).

of Scripture was made plain to my understanding and it was powerfully pressed home to me by the work of the Holy Spirit. The setting in a classroom may be quite different to a church, but the reception of biblical truth can be as forceful in it.[3]

d. *Always be connected with a local church fellowship and participate in its activities.* Monastic life is not the ideal way to carry out theological study. In the early church and in the Middle Ages this was considered the ideal, but escape into a monastery did not solve spiritual problems. Rather, it often created more. You need to learn in a setting where there is interaction with others, and also at the same time to be part of a local congregation and active in its life and ministry. A period of theological study should not separate you from the local church. It may mean that you have to restrict some of your church responsibilities owing to the demands of study, but it is best to try and retain as full an involvement locally as you can. Many aspects of theology will fall into place in your mind and heart as you study, participate in worship, and engage in other activities in your own church fellowship.

[3] For a classic discussion, B. B. Warfield, 'The Religious Life of Theological Students' (see Appendix 4 on p. 93 below). This was a pamphlet issued after Warfield gave the address at the annual conference at Princeton Theological Seminary in October 1911.

e. Build relationships with fellow students as these friendships last a lifetime and are often one of the best means of mutual encouragement in ministry. Fellow students should be a blessing to you during your years of study. You will interact with them and learn together, not just from your formal study material, but from their life experiences and on-going Christian commitment. There is no reason, however, why such deep friendships should not continue into the future, especially now that global communications make it so easy to keep in touch with friends.

6

Early Ministry

B EING called by a company of God's people is the proof of your gifts and also of the theological training that fits you for ministry. Whatever testing you have gone through along the way, the call to serve a particular congregation marks out in a special way the reality of fitness for ministry. This is why in most denominations ordination only occurs when such a call is issued and accepted. Ordination should not occur unless there is a definite field of service ahead.

Some pointers need to be given about early days in serving a congregation of God's people. Commencement of a new ministry is always an important time for both pastor and people. It should set the pattern for days to come, and, conversely, if you make glaring mistakes, you should learn from them and alter your patterns of service. Here are some things to bear in mind.

a. Realise afresh the immense privilege of being a pastor. What can be more important than ministering in the name of the Lord Jesus! You should be very aware of a sense of the fulfilment of God's calling in your life, and retain throughout it the main aim of ministry. Never forget that Christian ministry is a distinctive calling that is directed towards spiritual ends. That is why, in the Presbyterian tradition, one of the questions at the ordination or induction of a pastor is as follows: 'Are zeal for the glory of God, love to the Lord Jesus Christ, and a desire to save souls, and not worldly interests or expectations (so far as you know your own heart), your great motives and chief inducements to the work of the holy ministry?'

b. Build upon what you have learned in your theological course. There are many questions that will have arisen in your mind during your course of study. Now is the opportunity to return to them, and read up on them, and think them through. If you have done language study in your course, either Greek or Hebrew, or both, don't let the hard work and discipline you put into the study be dissipated. You may not become an expert in them, but many occasions will arise when you will be thankful that you can refer to the biblical text in the original languages. The content of some commentaries is only accessible to those with a knowledge of the languages. But never parade your knowledge of Greek and Hebrew in the pulpit. Other ways can easily be found to utilise a knowledge of the languages without drawing unnecessary attention to it. In the ministry you have to be continually reading, listening, and learning.[1]

c. See the need for planning your ministry. Structuring your time is necessary. It is easy to drop into undisciplined habits simply because you are not working in an environment where you are constrained by times set by others. You may well be alone in the work, and you have to organise your life so that you can accomplish all that must be done week-by-week. Of course, there will be interruptions to any programme you set up, and a week can see many unexpected events. This is simply part and parcel of ministry, and you must be able to adapt your plans to fit the circumstances. Get the aims right and always allot time for a variety of activities.

Fix certain time frames in the week. For example, if there are two Sunday services and one midweek, on Tuesday morning prepare for Sunday morning, on Wednesday prepare for the mid-week meeting, on Thurs-

---

[1] James Montgomery Boice has given some excellent autobiographical points about preaching and scholarship as well as wider discussion. See 'The Preacher and Scholarship' in Samuel T. Logan, Jr., *The Preacher and Preaching: Reviving the Art in the Twentieth Century*, pp. 91-104.

day prepare for Sunday evening. Come back at the end of the week and refresh what you have prepared, or add to it, especially illustrations. Preparing early in the week gives time to think over the biblical passage, reflect on its message, and clarify your own approach to the presentation of the message. Beware of leaving it too late in the week—and even on Saturday evening—to do your sermon preparation. Sermons produced under these circumstances have been called 'Saturday-night specials', also known as 'Tyndale Commentary sermons', because of dependence on one notable commentary series for the sermon content.

It is often helpful to write out a list of things that have to be done on a certain day or week. List all the phone calls you need to make, and start with the most difficult one. If that one is out of the way, your mind will be much clearer to get on with the rest of the calls. Watch, too, the time you spend on emails. My wife helpfully suggested some years ago that I do a morning of work in my study before I look at incoming emails. That has been good, and makes sure that I am not distracted from my study by messages intruding on my time and diverting me from my main work.

d. Though planning is needed, ministry does not always proceed in accordance with our plans. Pastoral needs will arise at odd times, not when you think they should. As a pastor, you are a servant of God and a servant of the flock. Hence, you need to be adaptable regarding your schedule as often it will require adjustment to meet pressing needs in the congregation. This simply reinforces the need for planning in order that pulpit and other preparation can be done in advance so that unusual circumstances do not disrupt your planned activities. Prepare for the unexpected! Do not let precious time go to waste!

e. Plan your preaching some months ahead. Good preaching requires good planning. You need to know the Christian maturity of your congregation and at what level you should pitch your preaching. It is always best to err on the side of simplicity and directness. Try and avoid being committed to very long series of expositions. These so often become tedious for the congregation, and a certain type of monotony creeps in. Try not to let a series run beyond eight or ten weeks without inserting some different topics into the programme. Don't think that because some of the Puritans or more recent prominent pastors preached for a year or longer on a particular book that this method should be slavishly followed by every preacher today.

It is hard to know how much of your preparation for preaching should be committed to paper. When I became a student I was advised to write out my sermons in full. I did that for a few years, taking only briefer notes into the pulpit. However, I found that practice was too stifling and time-consuming. I preferred to use less notes even in the pulpit so that I could maintain as much eye-contact with the congregation as possible. My sermon notes for years have been a single sheet with just the main outline set out. One feature I have found useful is to give more detail about any illustration I use so that I can locate the source if I want to use it again. My experience has been that if I do my preparation early in the week, I often have the main outline so fixed in my mind that I hardly need notes on the Sunday. Preachers have to work out what works best for them and for their hearers.

f. Remember that you have to cover a broad range of activities in the pastorate. If you make a list of all the varied duties, you will probably discover fairly quickly that you don't feel as equally comfortable in every one. However, in many congregations you will be expected to carry out many tasks as the pastor. You need to recognise where your strengths lie, but also your weaknesses. Some of your weaknesses may simply be the result of inexperience—you have never had to do certain tasks before. New activities will challenge you, but often after a period of time they will become familiar and you will feel comfortable in doing them. Learn from others and step out to develop your gifts in a wide area. Exercise an all-round ministry.[2] Systematic pastoral visiting, often with your wife or an office-bearer, always brings forth fruit as you get to know the needs of the congregation.

From the outset you have to realise that the work of a congregation doesn't depend on you alone. You have to be prepared to delegate responsibility to others. If there are not enough suitable people to carry out the tasks, look for those you can mentor and train. This is particularly important with regard to men who may well serve in the future as deacons or elders. The same applies to women who can be nurtured and encouraged by mature and gifted women in the congregation. Many roles outside of formal office within the church are available for women.

g. Learn to deal with difference of opinion and controversy. This is an area in which many pastors fail badly. There are always going to be differences of opinion among Christians. One only has to look at the New Testament epistles to see that. The Christians at Corinth were divided (1 Cor. 1:10-17), while in Philippi Syntyche and Euodia had to be encouraged to agree

[2] See the book by C. H. Spurgeon, *An All-Round Ministry* (Edinburgh: Banner of Truth, 1999).

with each other in the Lord (Phil. 4:2). I know I found it hard at first to go to someone and raise a difficult issue with them. In time I found it best to speak to someone on the phone, or, better still, face to face. I simply say that there is a matter that I want to speak with them about (naming the issue) and ask if we can fix a time for the conversation. When we do meet, I thank the person for making the time available to discuss the matter and immediately proceed to the issue in question.

h. Keep some time free in the week for general reading that has no direct relevance to your present ministry. You will need the stimulus from what you read. Some pastors become so directed in their preparation for their current preaching ministry that they fail to broaden their minds with wider reading. I suggest that you should set aside one morning a week for this, or else some other suitable time. Some suggest a half-an-hour of reading first thing in the morning before getting down to our other work for the day. I spent time teaching in a seminary in which most of my faculty colleagues did not stay around at lunch time. This meant I was free to devote myself for an hour every day to whatever books I wanted to read. I chose books normally outside my own teaching area, and, looking back, I covered a wide range of topics and found that much of that reading came in useful at later stages of my ministry.

i. From the outset decide on some special area of interest in theology or ministry. Make it a hobby that could later be of use to the wider church. One can think of pastors who have developed expertise in an area in which they particularly enjoy working, and this expertise can be called upon by the wider church. I can think of those who had an interest in an aspect of theology, or a period of church history, or in modern ethical questions. Such people are invaluable in the life of the church.

j. Try and have someone you can share with and pray with, preferably outside your congregation. This may be another pastor, or a mature Christian whom you trust, and who can keep confidences. This means you can speak freely about yourself and your ministry, raise problems you are facing, and seek advice as to appropriate action.

7

Staying Fresh

WHEN commencing ministry the normal intention is to carry on for years to come. It may be interrupted at times by illness or other circumstances that compel a temporary break from normal pastoral activities. Such a break should not suggest that ministerial work should thereafter be set aside, for even the prophet Elijah had to take time out to be refreshed and reinvigorated for further service (1 Kings 19:1-18). However, some positive plans can be put in place to help meet the pressures of ministry.

a. Understand that ministry will make heavy demands on you. It is taxing intellectually, emotionally, and physically. By its very nature, ministry involves hard work both in the study and in carrying out your responsibilities as a teacher and a pastor. You will be dealing constantly with people who have spiritual needs in addition to their temporal needs. Helping them can be draining, and if you are going to be able to be an effective shepherd of the flock of God you must reckon with the heavy burdens that you may have to carry. Supporting your fellow believers in all their varied life experiences can tax you immensely. We should not be surprised at how tiring ministry can be.[1]

b. Plan time with your family. Families often suffer because of the intrusion of pastoral demands. Sometimes this cannot be avoided, but at least you can be prepared for it. Your first priority has to be your own family, who need fatherly care and attention. Nothing can substitute for this, for if you cannot care for your family, how can you care for the church of God? (1 Tim. 3:5). You need also to refrain from discussing sensitive pastoral matters in front of family members, so that you preserve confidentiality, but also that you do not unnecessarily concern them with issues that are being dealt with by the church leadership.

---

[1] For wise advice on coping in the ministry, see Peter Brain, *Going the Distance: How to Stay Fit for a Lifetime of Ministry*, 2nd ed. (Sydney: Matthias Press, 2006). Chapters 12 and 13 have been printed as *Helping Your Pastor to Go the Distance: How Local Churches Can Help Their Pastors Stay Fit for a Lifetime of Ministry* (Armidale, N.S.W.: Diocese of Armidale, 2005).

c. Your spiritual life has to be nourished if you are going to provide spiritual food for others. What was said earlier about spiritual growth during your theological training, applies equally to your spiritual life as a pastor. If you are to feed others, you yourself must be fed from God's word. Paul's principle was that elders have to guard themselves, as well as guarding the flock of God (Acts 20:28). In preparing for preaching or teaching, you must be subject to the truth of God, and it must speak to your heart before you declare it to others. Likewise, you must realise that there are temptations in ministry and great care is needed less Satan deflect you in your obedience to Christ.[2]

d. Take your annual leave rather than accumulate it. Pastors need periods of relaxation and it is important to take a break from normal routines of ministry and to be refreshed. I have often found that not only a change in location helps, but also a change in reading. I often read things that I haven't time to read in the normal pressures of ministry. I usually try and have some heavier reading with me, as well as something lighter. Vacation time is convenient for being able to get

[2] Very helpful comments are made by Erroll Hulse on the minister's spiritual life. See, 'The Minister's Piety', in Samuel T. Logan, Jr., *The Preacher and Preaching: Reviving the Art in the Twentieth Century*, pp. 62-90.

into a solid volume without the normal interruptions and distractions. I have often advised students during their theological course to read in the summer vacation things like Arnold Dallimore's *George Whitfield*,[3] or Spurgeon's *Autobiography*,[4] or to work through Calvin's *Institutes*.[5] Some have found that more writing gets done on a vacation than at any other time. Everyone is different in their habits and needs, and hence none of us can be prescriptive for others.

e. Conferences will provide a special help to you when in ministry. Their stimulus is important, but a couple of caveats are necessary. Some pastors attend too many conferences, seemingly hoping that something from them will invigorate their ministry or provide new ideas for them to try. Attending too many conferences is time-consuming, expensive, and tiring. One goes to a conference to listen, but also to meet others of similar persuasions. This involves conversations that require mental attention and thought. Never look on conferences as a vacation. They are part of your study programme.

[3] Arnold Dallimore, *George Whitfield: The Life and Times of the Great Evangelist of the 18th Century Revival*, 2 vols. (Edinburgh: Banner of Truth, 1970, 1980).

[4] C. H. Spurgeon, *Autobiography*, 2 vols. (Edinburgh: Banner of Truth, 1974).

[5] John Calvin, *The Institutes of the Christian Religion, 1541 edition*, trans. Robert White (Edinburgh: Banner of Truth, 2014).

f. Set out as if your first congregation was going to be your only one. When you receive a call from a congregation and you accept, believing that God has opened this ministry to you, begin as if you were going to spend your whole ministry there. Give yourself to the work, not looking on it as if it was only going to be of short duration. Fresh study is needed to feed the sheep, and you have to start as you want to finish. Don't look on your first parish as if it was just a stepping stone to another larger, and perhaps more prestigious one. We need pastors who will settle in for the long haul.

Conclusion

MINISTRY in the name of Christ is a wonderful calling, but not one you can fulfil in your own strength. Without the aid of the Holy Spirit you will not achieve anything for the kingdom of God. Persuading people to lay hold of Christ does not depend upon your eloquence, but on the Spirit's power. Faith should 'not rest in the wisdom of men but in the power of God' (1 Cor. 2:5). Your calling is to faithfulness in your service as you preach not yourself but Christ Jesus as Lord. In doing so, you have to demonstrate that you are a servant for Jesus' sake in any congregation you serve (2 Cor. 4:5). Your calling is to be a shepherd of the church of God 'which he obtained with his own blood' (Acts 20:28).

Short Bibliography

L ISTED here are some books that you will find helpful, as they deal with many of the questions that I have covered in this book.

- Richard Baxter, *The Reformed Pastor* (Edinburgh: Banner of Truth, reprinted 1974).

- Peter Brain, *Going the Distance: How to Stay Fit for a Lifetime of Ministry*, 2nd ed. (Sydney: Matthias Press, 2006).

- Charles Bridges, *The Christian Ministry* (Edinburgh: Banner of Truth, reprinted 1976).

- Edmund Clowney, *Called to the Ministry* (Nutley, N.J.: Presbyterian and Reformed Publishing Company, 1964).

- Brian Croft, *Test, Train, Affirm and Send into Ministry: Recovering the Local Church's Responsibility in the External Call* (Leonminster: Day One, 2010).

• James M. Garretson, *Princeton and Preaching: Archibald Alexander and the Christian Ministry* (Edinburgh: Banner of Truth, 2004).

• William Guthrie, *The Christian's Great Interest* (Edinburgh: Banner of Truth, 1982).

• Samuel T. Logan, Jr., *The Preacher and Preaching: Reviving the Art in the Twentieth Century* (Phillipsburg, N.J.: Presbyterian and Reformed Publishing Company, 2011).

• John Piper and Don Carson, *The Pastor as Scholar and the Scholar as Pastor* (Wheaton: Crossway Publishing Company, 2011).

• John Piper, *Brothers, We Are Not Professionals: A Plea to Pastors for Radical Ministry* (Fearn: Christian Focus Publications, 2008).

• C. H. Spurgeon, *An All-Round Ministry* (Edinburgh: Banner of Truth, 1999).

• C. H. Spurgeon, *Lectures to My Students* (Edinburgh: Banner of Truth, 2008).

• Geoffrey Thomas, *Reading the Bible* (Edinburgh: Banner of Truth, 1981).

• B. B. Warfield, 'The Religious Life of Theological Students', in James M. Garretson, ed. *Princeton and the* Work *of the Christian Ministry*, vol. 2 (Edinburgh: Banner of Truth: 2012), p. 412-425, and in John E. Meeter, ed. *Selected Shorter Writings of Benjamin B. Warfield*—I (Nutley: Presbyterian and Reformed Publishing Company, 1970), pp. 411-425. (See Appendix 4 on p. 93 below.)

• Warren Wiersbe and David Wiersbe, *Making Sense of the Ministry: How to Apply Your Education to the Pastorate* (Grand Rapids: Baker Book House, 1983).

Appendix 1

Suggested Preparatory Reading

THE lists here give information on some books that you may find helpful as you commence theological study. They are grouped under various topics, and are graded in size and difficulty (1, 2, 3). If they are unobtainable new, copies can often be obtained secondhand, especially from internet sites. Try www.bookfinder.com, or www.usedbooksearch.net, or www.abebooks.com.

General Introduction to Theological Study

Kelly M. Kapic, *A Little Book for New Theologians: Why and How to Study Theology* (Downers Grove: IVP Academic, 2012).

Biblical Content and Biblical Theology

1. Sinclair B. Ferguson, *From the Mouth of God: Trusting, Reading and Applying the Bible* (Edinburgh: Banner of Truth, 2014).

Wayne Grudem, C. John Collins, and Thomas R. Schreiner, eds., *Understanding Scripture: An Overview of the Bible's Origin, Reliability, and Meaning* (Wheaton: Crossway, 2012).

2. Graeme Goldsworthy, *According To Plan: The Unfolding Revelation of God in the Bible* (Leicester: InterVarsity Press, 2001).

3. E. A. Martens, *God's Design: Focus on Old Testament Theology*, 3rd ed. (North Richland Hills, Texas: D. & F. Scott Publishing, 1998).

Church History

1. Iain D. Campbell, *Heroes and Heretics: Pivotal Moments in 20 Centuries of the Church* (Fearn: Christian Focus Publications, 2004).

2. A. M. Renwick and A. M. Harman, *The Story of the Church*, 3rd ed. (Nottingham: Inter-Varsity Press, 1996).

3. Bruce Shelley, *Church History in Plain Language*, 2nd ed. (Nashville: Thomas Nelson, 1996).

Theology

1. J. I. Packer, *Concise Theology: A Guide to Historic Christian Beliefs* (Nottingham: InterVarsity, 2011).

2. Bruce Milne, *Know the Truth: A Handbook of Christian Belief* (Nottingham: InterVarsity, 2010, 3rd ed.).

3. John Murray, *Redemption Accomplished and Applied* (Grand Rapids: Eerdmans, 1989; also Edinburgh: Banner of Truth, 2009).

Preaching

1. J. A. Motyer, *Preaching?: Simple Teaching on Simply Preaching* (Fearn: Christian Focus Publications, 2013).

2. John Piper, *The Supremacy of God in Preaching*, revised ed. (Grand Rapids: Baker Book House, 2004).

3. Samuel Logan Jr., ed., *The Preacher and Preaching: Reviving the Art in the Twentieth Century* (Nutley: Presbyterian and Reformed, 2011).

Christian Life

1. Sinclair B. Ferguson, *The Christian Life: A Doctrinal Introduction* (Edinburgh: Banner of Truth, 2013).

2. J. I. Packer, *Quest for Godliness: The Puritan Vision of the Christian Life* (Wheaton: Crossway, 1990).

3. J. C. Ryle, *Holiness: Its Nature, Hindrances, Difficulties, and Roots* (Edinburgh: Banner of Truth, 2015).

Philosophy and Apologetics

1. Richard Pratt, *Every Thought Captive: A Study Manual for the Defense of the Truth* (Nutley: Presbyterian and Reformed, 2012).

2. Scott Oliphant, *Covenantal Apologetics: Principles and Practice in Defense of Our Faith* (Wheaton: Crossway, 2013).

3. John Frame, *Apologetics to the Glory of God: An Introduction* (Nutley: Presbyterian and Reformed, 1994).

Evangelism

1. John Chapman, *Know and Tell the Gospel: The Why and How of Evangelism* (Sydney: Matthias Media, 1998).

2. R. B. Kuiper, *God-Centred Evangelism: A Presentation of the Scriptural Theology of Evangelism* (Edinburgh: Banner of Truth, 2012).

3. J. I. Packer, *Evangelism and the Sovereignty of God* (Nottingham: Inter-Varsity Press, 2010).

Appendix 2

A Short Guide to Sermon Preparation

1. Prayer

Pray over your choice of a passage. Avoid ones with obvious difficulties of interpretation and application.

Continue to seek the guidance and assistance of the Holy Spirit as you endeavour to understand the passage and prepare to explain it to others.

2. Read the passage carefully

2.1: Start with the English version you normally use, but then read the passage in one or two other versions, if you have them handy. Read silently at first, but then read aloud.

2.2: Check the section to make sure it is a unit in its own right.

3. Central theme of the passage

3.1: Write down the central theme as it appears from your examination of the passage.

3.2: If you cannot do this, then retrace steps 1-2, or else move to another passage. Do not proceed if you are unsure at this stage.

4. Historical, geographical and biblical context

4.1: Check the historical context in which the words were spoken; *e.g.*, see if a Davidic Psalm is linked with a particular period or episode in David's life, or check if a passage in one of Paul's epistles refers to an incident in his ministry as described in the Book of Acts.

4.2: If place names are mentioned, check them in a Bible atlas so you know where they are located, and if they have any special relevance for your message.

4.3: Be aware of the wider context of the passage in the biblical text, as it may relate to other incidents or to similar teaching.

5. Preliminary scheme for the sermon

5.1: Break up the main ideas of the passage and see if some outline starts to develop.

5.2: Check the important words or key ideas. If you have a Bible dictionary, it may have some helpful comments.

5.3: Be prepared to work over such a preliminary outline several times, and do not hesitate to change the scheme!

6. Sermon outline

6.1: Frame a general outline of the sermon under headings such as:

Theme:

Introduction:

1.

2.

3.

(4.)

Conclusion:

6.2: If you have access to commentaries on the passage, read them, and from them add notes to the outline you have prepared. The commentaries should be a check on any wayward interpretation you may have reached, and they will also provide additional information. Be careful you do not try and include in your sermon *every* detail you find in commentaries or your sermon will become overloaded with information.

7. Application and illustration

7.1: Assess the practical relevance of the content of your sermon for your hearers. Sometimes this can be done by putting it as a sentence: *At the end of the sermon we* [preacher and people] *should be praising God for ... [should respond like David by ...].*

7.2: All scriptural truth should ultimately have practical application, but do not try and press a passage in an artificial way.

7.3: Think of illustrations to reinforce particular points throughout the sermon, but remember, illustrations are meant to let in the light, not to be an end in themselves.

9. Final preparations

9.1: Do not do your sermon preparation hurriedly. Try and do the basic sermon preparation some days in advance of preaching.

9.2: Set aside your notes but continue to think and pray over the passage.

9.3: Other illustrations, or ways of expressing certain parts, will become clearer. Write down enough of the content, including the illustrations, so you can re-use the sermon at a later date.

9.4: Come back and revise your notes, paying particular attention to the introduction and conclusion of the sermon.

9.5: Keep in mind that preaching is meant to inform, but also, under God's blessing, to *move hearers to action*. The aim of preaching is to see sinners converted, and believers coming to maturity in Christ. Never lose sight of these twin aims.

Appendix 3

The Minister's Self-Watch[1]

Take heed unto thyself, and unto the doctrine.
1 Timothy 4:16

EVERY workman knows the necessity of keeping his tools in a good state of repair, for 'if the iron be blunt, and he do not whet the edge, then must he put to more strength'. If the workman lose the edge from his adze[2], he knows that there will be a greater draught upon his energies, or his work will be badly done. Michelangelo, the elect of the fine arts, understood so well the importance of his tools, that he always made his own brushes with his own hands, and in this he gives us an illustration of the God of grace, who with

---

[1] C. H. Spurgeon, *Lectures to My Students* (Edinburgh: Banner of Truth, 2008).
[2] adze: a cutting tool with an arched blade at right angles to the handle.

special care fashions for himself all true ministers. It is true that the Lord, like Quintin Matsys in the story of the Antwerp well-cover, can work with the faultiest kind of instrumentality, as he does when he occasionally makes very foolish preaching to be useful in conversion; and he can even work without agents, as he does when he saves men without a preacher at all, applying the Word directly by his Holy Spirit; but we cannot regard God's absolutely sovereign acts as a rule for our action. He may, in his own absoluteness, do as pleases him best, but we must act as his plainer dispensations instruct us; and one of the facts which is clear enough is this, that the Lord usually adapts means to ends, from which the plain lesson is, that we shall be likely to accomplish most when we are in the best spiritual condition; or in other words, we shall usually do our Lord's work best when our gifts and graces are in good order, and we shall do worst when they are most out of trim. This is a practical truth for our guidance; when the Lord makes exceptions, they do but prove the rule.

We are, in a certain sense, our own tools, and therefore must keep ourselves in order. If I want to preach the gospel, I can only use my own voice; therefore I must train my vocal powers. I can only think with my own brains, and feel with my own heart, and therefore I must educate my intellectual and emotional faculties. I can only weep and agonize for souls in my own renewed nature; therefore must I watchfully maintain the tenderness which was in Christ Jesus. It will be in vain for me to stock my library, or organize societies, or project schemes, if I neglect the culture of myself; for books, and agencies, and systems, are only remotely the instruments of my holy calling; my own spirit, soul, and body, are my nearest machinery for sacred service; my spiritual faculties, and my inner life, are my battle axe and weapons of war. M'Cheyne, writing to a ministerial friend, who was travelling with a view to perfecting himself in the German tongue, used language identical with our own:

> I know you will apply hard to German, but do not forget the culture of the inner man — I mean of the heart. How diligently the cavalry officer keeps his sabre clean and sharp; every stain he rubs off with the greatest care. Remember you are God's sword, his instrument — I trust, a chosen vessel unto him to bear his name. In great measure, according to the purity and perfection of the instrument, will be the success. It is not great talents God blesses so much as likeness to Jesus. A holy minister is an awful weapon in the hand of God.

For the herald of the gospel to be spiritually out of order in his own proper person is, both to himself and to his work, a most serious calamity; and yet, my brethren, how easily is such an evil produced, and with what watchfulness must it be guarded against! Travelling one day by express from Perth to Edinburgh, on a sudden we came to a dead stop, because a very small screw in one of the engines — every railway locomotive consisting virtually of two engines — had been broken, and when we started again we were obliged to crawl along with one piston-rod at work instead of two. Only a small screw was gone, if that had been right the train would have rushed along its iron road, but the absence of that insignificant piece of iron disarranged the whole. A train is said to have been stopped on one of the United States' railways by flies in the grease-boxes of the carriage wheels. The analogy is perfect; a man in all other respects fitted to be useful, may by some small defect be exceedingly hindered, or even rendered utterly useless. Such a result is all the more grievous, because it is associated with the gospel, which in the highest sense is adapted to effect the grandest results. It is a terrible thing when the healing balm loses its efficacy through the blunderer who administers it. You all know the injurious effects frequently produced upon water through flowing along leaden pipes; even so the gospel itself, in flowing through men who are spiritually unhealthy, may be debased until it grows injurious to their hearers. It is to be feared that Calvinistic doctrine becomes most evil teaching when it is set forth by men of ungodly lives, and exhibited as if it were a cloak for licentiousness; and Arminianism, on the other hand, with its wide sweep of the offer of mercy, may do most serious damage to the souls of men, if the careless tone of the preacher leads his hearers to believe that they *can* repent whenever they please; and that, therefore, no urgency surrounds the gospel message.

Moreover, when a preacher is poor in grace, any lasting good which may be the result of his ministry, will usually be feeble and utterly out of proportion with what might have been expected. Much sowing will be followed by little reaping; the interest upon the talents will be inappreciably small. In two or three of the battles which were lost in the late American war, the result is said to have been due to the bad gunpowder which was served out by certain 'shoddy' contractors to the army, so that the due effect of a cannonade was not produced. So it may be with us. We may miss our mark, lose our end and aim, and waste our time, through not possessing true vital force within ourselves, or not possessing it in such a degree that God could consistently bless us. Beware of being 'shoddy' preachers.

1. *It should be one of our first cares that we ourselves be saved men.*

That a teacher of the gospel should first be a partaker of it is a simple truth, but at the same time a rule of the most weighty importance. We are not among those who accept the apostolical succession of young men simply because they assume it; if their college experience has been rather vivacious than spiritual, if their honours have been connected rather with athletic exercises than with labours for Christ, we demand evidence of another kind than they are able to present to us. No amount of fees paid to learned doctors, and no amount of classics received in return, appear to us to be evidences of a call from above. True and genuine piety is necessary as the first indispensable requisite; whatever 'call' a man may pretend to have, if he has not been called to holiness, he certainly has not been called to the ministry. 'First be trimmed thyself, and then adorn thy brother', say the rabbins. 'The hand', saith Gregory, 'that means to make another clean, must not itself be dirty.' If your salt be unsavoury how can you season others? Conversion is a *sine qua non* in a minister. Ye aspirants to our pulpits, 'ye must be born again.' Nor is the possession of this first qualification a thing to be taken for granted by any man, for there is very great possibility of our being mistaken as to whether we are converted or not. Believe me, it is no child's play to 'make your calling and election sure'. The world is full of counterfeits, and swarms with panderers to carnal self-conceit, who gather around a minister as vultures around a carcass. Our own hearts are deceitful, so that truth lies not on the surface, but must be drawn up from the deepest well. We must search ourselves very anxiously and very thoroughly, lest by any means after having preached to others we ourselves should be cast-aways.

How horrible to be a preacher of the gospel and yet to be unconverted! Let each man here whisper to his own inmost soul, 'What a dreadful thing it will be for me if I should be ignorant of the power of the truth which I am preparing to proclaim!' Unconverted ministry involves the most unnatural relationships. A graceless pastor is a blind man elected to a professorship of optics, philosophizing upon light and vision, discoursing upon and distinguishing to others the nice shades and delicate blendings of the prismatic colours, while he himself is absolutely in the dark! He is a dumb man elevated to the chair of music; a deaf man fluent upon symphonies and harmonies! He is a mole professing to educate eaglets; a limpet elected to preside over angels. To such a relationship one might apply the most absurd and grotesque metaphors, except that the subject is too solemn. It is a dreadful position for a man to stand in, for he has undertaken a work for which he is totally, wholly, and altogether unqualified, but from the responsibilities of which this unfitness will not screen him, because he wilfully incurred them. Whatever his natural gifts, whatever his mental powers may be, he is utterly out of court for spiritual work if he has no spiritual life; and it is his duty to cease the ministerial office till he has received this first and simplest of qualifications for it.

Unconverted ministry must be equally dreadful in another respect. If the man has no commission, what a very *unhappy* position for him to occupy! What can he see in the experience of his people to give him comfort? How must he feel when he hears the cries of penitents; or listens to their anxious doubts and solemn fears? He must be astonished to think that his words should be owned to that end! The word of an unconverted man may be blessed to the conversion of souls, since the Lord, while he disowns the man, will still honour his own truth. How perplexed such a man must be when he is consulted concerning the difficulties of mature Christians! In the pathway of experience, in which his own regenerate hearers are led, he must feel himself quite at a loss. How can he listen to their deathbed joys, or join in their rapturous fellowships around the table of their Lord?

In many instances of young men put to a trade which they cannot endure, they have run away to sea sooner than follow an irksome business; but where shall that man flee who is apprenticed for life to this holy calling, and yet is a total stranger to the power of godliness? How can he daily bid men come to Christ, while he himself is a stranger to his dying love? O sirs, surely this must be perpetual slavery. Such a man must hate the sight of a pulpit as much as a galley-slave hates the oar.

And *how unserviceable* such a man must be. He has to guide travellers along a road which he has never trodden, to navigate a vessel along a coast of which he knows none of the landmarks! He is called to instruct others, being himself a fool. What can he be but a cloud without rain, a tree with leaves only. As when the caravan in the wilderness, all athirst and ready to die beneath the broiling sun, comes to the long desired well, and, horror of horrors! finds it without a drop of water; so when souls thirsting after God come to a graceless ministry, they are ready to perish because the water of life is not to be found. Better abolish pulpits than fill them with men who have no experimental knowledge of what they teach.

Alas! *the unregenerate pastor becomes terribly mischievous* too, for of all the causes which create infidelity, ungodly ministers must be ranked among the first. I read the other day, that no phase of evil presented so marvellous a power for destruction, as the unconverted minister of a parish, with a £1,200 organ, a choir of ungodly singers, and an aristocratic congregation. It was the opinion of the writer, that there could be no greater instrument for damnation out of hell than that. People go to their place of worship and sit down comfortably, and think they must be Christians, when all the time all that their religion consists in, is listening to an orator, having their ears tickled with music, and perhaps their eyes amused with graceful action and fashionable manners; the whole being no better than what they hear and see at the opera — not so good, perhaps, in point of aesthetic beauty, and not an atom more spiritual. Thousands are congratulating themselves, and even blessing God that they are devout worshippers, when at the same time they are living in an unregenerate Christless state, having the form of godliness, but denying the power thereof. He who presides over a system which aims at nothing higher than formalism, is far more a servant of the devil than a minister of God.

A formal preacher is mischievous while he preserves his outward equilibrium, but as he is without the preserving balance of godliness, sooner or later he is almost sure to make a trip in his moral character, and what a position is he in then! How is God blasphemed, and the gospel abused!

Terrible is it to consider *what a death must await such a man! and what must be his after-condition!* The prophet pictures the king of Babylon going down to hell, and all the kings and princes whom he had destroyed, and whose capitals he had laid waste, rising up from their places in Pandemonium, and saluting the fallen tyrant with the cutting sarcasm, 'Art thou become like unto us?' And cannot you suppose a man who has been a minister, but who has lived without Christ in his heart, going down to hell, and all the imprisoned spirits who used to hear him, and all the ungodly of his parish rising up and saying to him in bitter tones, 'Art thou also become as we are? Physician, didst thou not heal thyself? Art thou who claimed to be a shining light cast down into the darkness for ever?' Oh! if one must be lost, let it not be in this fashion! To be lost under the shadow of a pulpit is dreadful, but how much more so to perish from the pulpit itself! There is an awful passage in John Bunyan's treatise, entitled *Sighs from Hell,* which full often rings in my ears:

> How many souls have blind priests been the means of destroying by their ignorance? Preaching that was no better for their souls than rats-bane to the body. Many of them, it is to be feared, have whole

towns to answer for. Ah! friend, I tell thee, thou
that hast taken in hand to preach to the people, it
may be thou hast taken in hand thou canst not tell
what. Will it not grieve thee to see thy whole parish come bellowing after thee into hell, crying out,
'This we have to thank thee for, thou wast afraid
to tell us of our sins, lest we should not put meat
fast enough into thy mouth. O cursed wretch, who
wast not content, blind guide as thou wast, to fall
into the ditch thyself, but hast also led us thither
with thee.'

Richard Baxter, in his *Reformed Pastor*, amid much
other solemn matter, writes as follows:

Take heed to yourselves lest you should be void of
that saving grace of God which you offer to others, and be strangers to the effectual working of
that gospel which you preach; and lest, while you
proclaim the necessity of a Saviour to the world,
your hearts should neglect him, and you should
miss of an interest in him and his saving benefits.
Take heed to yourselves, lest you perish while you
call upon others to take heed of perishing, and
lest you famish yourselves while you prepare their
food. Though there be a promise of shining as stars
to those that turn many to righteousness (Daniel

12:3), this is but on supposition that they be first turned to it themselves: such promises are made *ceteris paribus, et suppositis supponendis.* Their own sincerity in the faith is the condition of their glory simply considered, though their great ministerial labours may be a condition of the promise of their greater glory. Many men have warned others that they come not to that place of torment, which yet they hasted to themselves; many a preacher is now in hell, that hath an hundred times called upon his hearers to use the utmost care and diligence to escape it. Can any reasonable man imagine that God should save men for offering salvation to others, while they refused it themselves, and for telling others those truths which they themselves neglected and abused? Many a tailor goes in rags that maketh costly clothes for others; and many a cook scarce licks his fingers, when he hath dressed for others the most costly dishes. Believe it, brethren, God never saved any man for being a preacher, nor because he was an able preacher; but because he was a justified, sanctified man, and consequently faithful in his Master's work. Take heed, therefore, to yourselves first, that you be that which you persuade others to be, and believe that which you persuade them daily to believe, and have heartily entertained that Christ and Spirit which you offer unto others. He that bade you love your neighbours as yourselves, did imply that you should love yourselves and not hate and destroy both yourselves and them.

My brethren, let these weighty sentences have due effect upon you. Surely there can be no need to add more; but let me pray you to examine yourselves, and so make good use of what has been addressed to you.

This first matter of true religion being settled,

2. It is of the next importance to the minister that his piety be vigorous.

He is not to be content with being equal to the rank and file of Christians, he must be a mature and advanced believer; for the ministry of Christ has been truly called 'the choicest of his choice, the elect of his election, a church picked out of the church'. If he were called to an ordinary position, and to common work, common grace might perhaps satisfy him, though even then it would be an indolent satisfaction; but being elect to extraordinary labours, and called to a place of unusual peril, he should be anxious to possess that superior strength which alone is adequate to his station. His pulse of vital godliness must beat strongly and regularly; his eye of faith must be bright; his foot of resolution must be firm; his hand of activity must be quick; his whole inner man must be in the highest degree of sanity. It is said of the Egyptians that they chose their priests from the most learned of their philosophers, and then they esteemed their priests so highly, that they chose their kings from them. We require to have for God's ministers the pick of all the Christian host; such men indeed, that if the nation wanted kings they could not do better than elevate them to the throne. Our weakest-minded, most timid, most carnal, and most ill-balanced men are not suitable candidates for the pulpit. There are some works which we should never allot to the invalid or deformed. A man may not be qualified for climbing lofty buildings, his brain may be too weak, and elevated work might place him in great danger; by all means let him keep on the ground and find useful occupation where a steady brain is less important: there are brethren who have analogous spiritual deficiencies, they cannot be called to service which is conspicuous and elevated, because their heads are too weak. If they were permitted a little success they would be intoxicated with vanity — a vice all too common among ministers, and of all things the least becoming in them, and the most certain to secure them a fall. Should we as a nation be called to defend our hearths and homes, we should not send out our boys and girls with swords and guns to meet the foe, neither may the church send out every fluent novice or inexperienced zealot to plead for the faith. The fear of the Lord must teach the young man wisdom, or he is barred from the pastorate; the grace of God must mature his spirit, or he had better tarry till power be given him from on high.

The highest moral character must be sedulously maintained. Many are disqualified for office in the church who are well enough as simple members. I hold very stern opinions with regard to Christian men who have fallen into gross sin; I rejoice that they may be truly converted, and may be with mingled hope and caution received into the church; but I question, gravely question, whether a man who has grossly sinned should be very readily restored to the pulpit. As John Angell James remarks, 'When a preacher of righteousness has stood in the way of sinners, he should never again open his lips in the great congregation until his repentance is as notorious as his sin.' Let those who have been shorn by the sons of Ammon tarry at Jericho till their beards be grown; this has often been used as a taunt to beardless boys to whom it is evidently inapplicable; it is an accurate enough metaphor for dishonoured and characterless men, let their age be what it may. Alas! the beard of reputation once shorn is hard to grow again. Open immorality, in most cases, however deep the repentance, is a fatal sign that ministerial graces were never in the man's character. Caesar's wife must be beyond suspicion, and there must be no ugly rumours as to ministerial inconsistency in the past, or the hope of usefulness will be slender. Into the church such fallen ones are to be received as penitents, and into the ministry they may be received if God puts them there; my doubt is not about that, but as to whether God ever did place them there; and my belief is that we should be very slow to help back to the pulpit men, who having been once tried, have proved themselves to have too little grace to stand the crucial test of ministerial life.

For some work we choose none but the strong; and when God calls us to ministerial labour we should endeavour to get grace that we may be strengthened into fitness for our position, and not be mere novices carried away by the temptations of Satan, to the injury of the church and our own ruin. We are to stand equipped with the whole armour of God, ready for feats of valour not expected of others: to us self-denial, self-forgetfulness, patience, perseverance, longsuffering, must be every-day virtues, and who is sufficient for these things? We had need live very near to God, if we would approve ourselves in our vocation.

Recollect, as ministers, that your whole life, your whole pastoral life especially, will be affected by the vigour of your piety. If your zeal grows dull, you will not pray well in the pulpit; you will pray worse in the family, and worst in the study alone. When your soul becomes lean, your hearers, without knowing how or why, will find that your prayers in public have little savour for them; they will feel your barrenness, perhaps, before you perceive it yourself. Your discourses will next betray your declension. You may utter as well-chosen words, and as fitly-ordered sentences, as aforetime; but there will be a perceptible loss of spiritual force. You will shake yourselves as at other times, even as Samson did, but you will find that your great strength has departed. In your daily communion with your people, they will not be slow to mark the all-pervading decline of your graces. Sharp eyes will see the grey hairs here and there long before you do. Let a man be afflicted with a disease of the heart, and all evils are wrapped up in that one — stomach, lungs, viscera, muscles, and nerves will all suffer; and so let a man have his heart weakened in spiritual things, and very soon his entire life will feel the withering influence. Moreover, as the result of your own decline, everyone of your hearers will suffer more or less; the vigorous amongst them will overcome the depressing tendency, but the weaker sort will be seriously damaged. It is with us and our hearers as it is with watches and the public clock; if our watch be wrong, very few will be misled by it but ourselves; but if the Horse Guards or Greenwich Observatory should go amiss, half London would lose its reckoning. So is it with the minister; he is the parish-clock, many take their time from him, and if he be incorrect, then they all go wrongly, more or less, and he is in a great measure accountable for all the sin which he occasions. This we cannot endure to think of, my brethren. It will not bear a moment's comfortable consideration, and yet it must be looked at that we may guard against it.

You must remember, too, that we have need of very vigorous piety, *because our danger is so much greater than that of others*. Upon the whole, no place is so assailed with temptation as the ministry. Despite the popular idea that ours is a snug retreat from temptation, it is *no less* true that our dangers are more numerous and more insidious than those of ordinary Christians. Ours may be a vantage-ground for height, but that height is perilous, and to many the ministry has proved a Tarpeian rock. If you ask what these temptations are, time might fail us to particularize them; but among them are both the coarser and the more refined; the courser are such temptations as self-indulgence at the table, enticements to which are superabundant among a hospitable people; the temptations of the flesh, which are incessant with young unmarried men set on high among an admiring throng of young women: but enough of this, your own observation will soon reveal to you a thousand snares, unless indeed your eyes are blinded. There are more secret snares than these, from which we can less easily escape; and of these the worst is the temptation to ministerialism — the tendency to read our Bibles as ministers, to pray as ministers, to get into doing the whole of our religion as not ourselves personally, but only relatively, concerned in it. To lose the personality of repentance and faith is a loss indeed. 'No man', says John Owen, 'preaches his sermon well to others if he doth not first preach it to his own heart.' Brethren, it is eminently hard to keep to this. Our office, instead of helping our piety, as some assert, is through the evil of our natures turned into one of its most serious hindrances; at least, I find it so. How one kicks and struggles against officialism, and yet how easily doth it beset us, like a long garment which twists around the racer's feet and impedes his running! Beware, dear brethren, of this and all the other seductions of your calling; and if you have done so until now, continue still to watch till life's latest hour.

We have noted but one of the perils, but indeed they are legion. The great enemy of souls takes care to leave no stone unturned for the preacher's ruin. 'Take heed to yourselves', says Baxter, because the tempter will make his first and sharpest onset upon you. If you will be the leaders against him, he will spare you no further than God restraineth him. He beareth you the greatest malice that are engaged to do him the greatest mischief. As he hateth Christ more than any of us, because he is the General of the field, and the 'Captain of our salvation', and doth more than all the world besides against the kingdom of darkness; so doth he note the leaders under him more than the common soldiers, on the like account, in their proportion. He knows what a rout he may make among the rest, if the leaders fall before their eyes. He hath long tried that way of fighting, 'neither with small nor great', comparatively, but these; and of 'smiting the shepherds, that he may scatter the flock'. And so great has been his success this way, that he will follow it on as far as he is able. Take heed, therefore, brethren, for the enemy hath a special eye upon you. You shall have his most subtle insinuations, and incessant solicitations, and violent assaults. As wise and learned as you are, take heed to yourselves lest he overwit you. The devil is a greater scholar than you, and a nimbler disputant; he can 'transform himself into an angel of light' to deceive, he will get within you and trip up your heels before you are aware; he will play the juggler with you undiscerned, and cheat you of your faith or innocency, and you shall not know that you have lost it: nay, he will make you believe it is multiplied or increased when it is lost. You shall see neither hook nor line, much less the subtle angler himself, while he is offering you his bait. And his baits shall be so fitted to your temper and disposition, that he will be sure to find advantages within you, and make your own principles and inclinations to betray you; and whenever he ruineth you, he will make you the instrument of your own ruin. Oh, what a conquest will he think he hath got, if he can make a minister lazy and unfaithful; if he can tempt a minister into covetousness or scandal! He will glory against the church, and say, 'These are your holy preachers: you see what their preciseness is, and whither it will bring them.' He will glory against Jesus Christ himself, and say, 'These are thy champions! I can make thy chiefest servants to abuse thee; I can make the stewards of thy house unfaithful.' If he did so insult against God upon a false surmise, and tell him he could make Job to curse him to his face (Job 1:2), what would he do if he should indeed prevail against us? And at last he will insult as much over you that ever he could draw you to be false to your great trust, and to blemish your holy profession, and to do him so much service that was your enemy. O do not so far gratify Satan; do not make him so much sport: suffer him not to use you as the Philistines did Samson — first to deprive you of your strength, and then to put out your eyes, and so to make you the matter of his triumph and derision.

Once more. We must cultivate the highest degree of godliness *because our work imperatively requires it.* The labour of the Christian ministry is well performed in exact proportion to the vigour of our renewed nature. Our work is only well done when it is well with ourselves. As is the workman, such will the work be. To face the enemies of truth, to defend the bulwarks of the faith, to rule well in the house of God, to comfort all that mourn, to edify the saints, to guide the perplexed, to bear with the froward, to win and nurse souls — all these and a thousand other works beside are not for a Feeble-mind or a Ready-to-halt, but are reserved for Great-heart whom the Lord has made strong for himself. Seek then strength from the Strong One, wisdom from the Wise One, in fact, all from the God of all.

3. Thirdly, let the minister take care that his personal character agrees in all respects with his ministry.

We have all heard the story of the man who preached so well and lived so badly, that when he was in the pulpit everybody said he ought never to come out again, and when he was out of it they all declared he never ought to enter it again. From the imitation of such a Janus may the Lord deliver us. May we never be priests of God at the altar, and sons of Belial outside the tabernacle door; but on the contrary, may we, as Nazianzen says of Basil, 'thunder in our doctrine, and lighten in our conversation'. We do not trust those persons who have two faces, nor will men believe in those whose verbal and practical testimonies are contradictory. As actions, according to the proverb, speak louder than words, so an ill life will effectually drown the voice of the most eloquent ministry. After all, our truest building must be performed with our hands; our characters must be more persuasive than our speech. Here I would not alone warn you of sins of commission, but of sins of omission. Too many preachers forget to serve God when they are out of the pulpit, their lives are negatively inconsistent. Abhor, dear brethren, the thought of being clockwork ministers who are not alive by abiding grace within, but are wound up by temporary influences; men who are only ministers for the time being, under the stress of the hour of ministering, but cease to be ministers when they descend the pulpit stairs. True ministers are always ministers. Too many preachers are like those sand-toys we buy for our children; you turn the box upside down, and the little acrobat revolves and revolves till the sand is all run down, and then he hangs motionless; so there are some who persevere in the ministrations of truth as long as there is an official necessity for their work, but after that, no pay, no paternoster; no salary, no sermon.

It is a horrible thing to be an inconsistent minister. Our Lord is said to have been like Moses, for this reason, that he was 'a prophet mighty in word and in deed'. The man of God should imitate his Master in this; he should be mighty both in the word of his doctrine and in the deed of his example, and mightiest, if possible, in the second. It is remarkable that the only church history we have is, 'The *Acts* of the Apostles'. The Holy Spirit has not preserved their sermons. They were very good ones, better than we shall ever preach, but still the Holy Spirit has only taken care of their 'acts'. We have no books of the resolutions of the apostles; when we hold our church-meetings we record our minutes and resolutions, but the Holy Spirit only puts down the 'acts'. Our acts should be such as to bear recording, for recorded they will be. We must live as under the more immediate eye of God, and as in the blaze of the great all-revealing day.

Holiness in a minister is at once his chief necessity and his goodliest ornament. Mere moral excellence is not enough, there must be the higher virtue; a consistent character there must be, but this must be anointed with the sacred consecrating oil, or that which makes us most fragrant to God and man will be wanting. Old John Stoughton, in his treatise entitled *The Preacher's Dignity and Duty*, insists upon the minister's holiness in sentences full of weight:

> If Uzzah must die but for *touching the ark of God,* and that to stay it when it was like to fall; if the men of Beth-shemesh for *looking into it*; if the very beasts that do but come near the holy mount be threatened; then what manner of persons ought they to be who shall be admitted to talk with God familiarly, to 'stand before him,' as the angels do, and 'behold his face continually'; 'to bear the ark upon their shoulders', 'to bear his name before the Gentiles'; in a word, to be his ambassadors? 'Holiness becometh thy house, O Lord'; and were it not a ridiculous thing to imagine, that the vessels must be holy, the vestures must be holy, all must be holy, but only he upon whose very garments must be written 'holiness to the Lord', might be

unholy; that the bells of the horses should have an inscription of holiness upon them, in Zechariah, and the saints' bells, the bells of Aaron, should be unhallowed? No, they must be 'burning and shining lights', or else their influence will dart some malignant quality; they must 'chew the cud and divide the hoof', or else they are unclean; they must 'divide the word aright', and walk uprightly in their life, and so join life to learning. If holiness be wanting, the ambassadors dishonour the country from whence they come, and the prince from whom they come; and this dead Amasa, this dead doctrine not quickened with a good life, lying in the way, stops the people of the Lord, that they cannot go on cheerfully in their spiritual warfare.'

The life of the preacher should be a magnet to draw men to Christ, and it is sad indeed when it keeps them from him. Sanctity in ministers is a loud call to sinners to repent, and when allied with holy cheerfulness it becomes wondrously attractive. Jeremy Taylor in his own rich language tell us,

Herod's doves could never have invited so many strangers to their dovecotes, if they had not been besmeared with opobalsamum: but, said Didymus; 'make your pigeons smell sweet, and they will allure whole flocks'; and if your life be excellent, if your virtues be like a precious ointment, you will soon invite your charges to run '*in odorem unguentorum*,' 'after your precious odours': but you must be excellent, not '*tanquam unus de populo*', *but* '*tanquam homo Dei*'; you must be a man of God, not after the common manner of men, but 'after God's own heart'; and men will strive to be like you, if you be like to God: but when you only stand at the door of virtue, for nothing but to keep sin out, you will draw into the folds of Christ none but such as fear drives in. '*Ad majorem Dei gloriam*', 'To do what will most glorify God', that is the line you must walk by: for to do no more than all men needs must is servility, not so much as the affection of sons; much less can you be fathers to the people, when you go not so far as the sons of God: for a dark lantern, though there be a weak brightness on one side, will scarce enlighten one, much less will it conduct a multitude, or allure many followers by the brightness of its flame.

Another equally admirable episcopal divine[31] has well and pithily said:

[3] Bishop Reynolds.

The star which led the wise men unto Christ, the pillar of fire which led the children unto Canaan, did not only shine, but go before them. (Matthew 2:9; Exodus 13:21.) The voice of Jacob will do little good if the hands be the hands of Esau. In the law, no person who had any blemish was to offer the oblations of the Lord (Leviticus 21:17–20); the Lord thereby teaching us what graces ought to be in his ministers. The priest was to have in his robes bells and pomegranates; the one a figure of sound doctrine, and the other of a fruitful life (Exodus 28:33–34). The Lord will be sanctified in all those that draw near unto him (Isaiah 52:11); for the sins of the priests make the people abhor the offering of the Lord (1 Samuel 2:17); their wicked lives do shame their doctrine; *Passionem Christi annunciant profitendo, male agendo exhonorant,* as St Austin speaks: with their doctrine they build, and with their lives they destroy. I conclude this point with that wholesome passage of *Hierom ad Nepotianum.* Let not, saith he, thy works shame thy doctrine, lest they who hear thee in the church tacitly answer, Why doest thou not thyself what thou teachest to others? He is too delicate a teacher who persuadeth others to fast with a full belly. A robber may accuse covetousness. *Sacerdotis*

Christi os, mens, manusque concordent; a minister of Christ should have his tongue, and his heart, and his hand agree.

Very quaint also is the language of Thomas Playfere in his *Say Well, Do Well*:

There was a ridiculous actor in the city of Smyrna, who, pronouncing O *coelum!* O heaven! pointed with his finger towards the ground; which when Polemo, the chiefest man in the place, saw, he could abide to stay no longer, but went from the company in a great chafe, saying, 'This fool hath made a solecism with his hand, he has spoken false Latin with his finger.' And such are they who *teach* well and *do* ill; that however they have *heaven* at their tongue's end, yet the *earth* is at their finger's end; such as do not only speak false Latin with their tongue, but false divinity with their hands; such as live not according to their preaching. But he that sits in the heaven will laugh them to scorn, and hiss them off the stage, if they do not mend their action.

Even in little things the minister should take care that his life is consistent with his ministry. He should be especially careful never to fall short of his word. This should be pushed even to scrupulosity; we cannot be too careful; truth must not only be in us, but shine from us. A celebrated doctor of divinity in London, who is now in heaven I have no doubt — a very excellent and godly man — gave notice one Sunday that he intended to visit all his people, and said, that in order to be able to get round and visit them and their families once in the year, he should take all the seat-holders in order. A person well known to me, who was then a poor man, was delighted with the idea that the minister was coming to his house to see him, and about a week or two before he conceived it would be his turn, his wife was very careful to sweep the hearth and keep the house tidy, and the man ran home early from work, hoping each night to find the doctor there. This went on for a considerable time. He either forgot his promise, or grew weary in performing it, or for some other reason never went to this poor man's house, and the result was this, the man lost confidence in all preachers, and said, 'They care for the rich, but they do not care for us who are poor.' That man never settled down to any one place of worship for many years, till at last he dropped into Exeter Hall and remained my hearer for years till providence removed him. It was no small task to make him believe that any minister could be an honest man, and could impartially love both rich and poor. Let us avoid doing such mischief, by being very particular as to our word.

We must remember that we are very much looked at. Men hardly have the impudence to break the law in the open sight of their fellows, yet in such publicity we live and move. We are watched by a thousand eagle eyes; let us so act that we shall never need to care if all heaven, and earth, and hell, swelled the list of spectators. Our public position is a great gain if we are enabled to exhibit the fruits of the Spirit in our lives; take heed, brethren, that you throw not away the advantage.

When we say to you, my dear brethren, take care of your life, we mean be careful of even the minutiae of your character. Avoid little debts, unpunctuality, gossiping, nicknaming, petty quarrels, and all other of those little vices which fill the ointment with flies. The self-indulgences which have lowered the repute of many must not be tolerated by us. The familiarities which have laid others under suspicion, we must chastely avoid. The roughnesses which have rendered some obnoxious, and the fopperies which have made others contemptible, we must put away. We cannot afford to run great risks through little things. Our care must be to act on the rule, 'giving no offence in anything, that the ministry be not blamed.'

By this is not intended that we are to hold ourselves bound by every whim or fashion of the society in which we move. As a general rule I hate the fashions of society, and detest conventionalities, and if I conceived it best to put my foot through a law of etiquette, I should feel gratified in having it to do. No, we are men, not slaves; and are not to relinquish our manly freedom, to be the lackeys of those who affect gentility or boast refinement. Yet, brethren, anything that verges upon the coarseness which is akin to sin, we must shun as we would a viper. The rules of Chesterfield are ridiculous to us, but not the example of Christ; and he was never coarse, low, discourteous, or indelicate.

Even in your recreations, remember that you are ministers. When you are off the parade you are still officers in the army of Christ, and as such demean yourselves. But if the lesser things must be looked after, how careful should you be in the great matters of morality, honesty, and integrity! Here the minister must not fail. His private life must ever keep good tune with his ministry, or his day will soon set with him, and the sooner he retires the better, for his continuance in his office will only dishonour the cause of God and ruin himself.

Brethren, the limits of a lecture are reached, and we must adjourn.

Appendix 4

The Religious Life of Theological Students[1]

A minister must be both learned and religious. It is not a matter of choosing between the two. He must study, but he must study as in the presence of God and not in a secular spirit. He must recognize the privilege of pursuing his studies in the environment where God and salvation from sin are the air he breathes. He must also take advantage of every opportunity for corporate worship, particularly while he trains in the theological seminary. Christ himself leads in setting the example of the importance of participating in corporate expressions of the religious life of the community. Ministerial work without taking time to pray is a tragic mistake. The two must combine if the servant of God is to give a pure, clear, and strong message.

[1] B. B. Warfield, 'The Religious Life of Theological Students', (no publisher, 1911). The prefatory abstract (the first paragraph) is an editorial addition to the original article.

PREPARATION FOR MINISTRY

* * * * *

I am asked to speak to you on the religious life of the student of theology. I approach the subject with some trepidation. I think it the most important subject which can engage our thought. You will not uspect me, in saying this, to be depreciating the importance of the intellectual preparation of the student for the ministry. The importance of the intellectual preparation of the student for the ministry is the reason of the existence of our theological seminaries. Say what you will, do what you will, the ministry is a 'learned profession'; and the man without learning, no matter with what other gifts he may be endowed, is unfit for its duties. But learning, though indispensable, is not the most indispensable thing for a minister. 'Apt to teach'—yes, the ministry must be 'apt to teach'; and observe that what I say—or rather what Paul says—is 'apt to teach'. Not apt merely to exhort, to beseech, to appeal, to entreat; nor even merely, to testify, to bear witness; but to teach. And teaching implies knowledge: he who teaches must know. Paul, in other words, requires of you, as we are perhaps learning not very felicitously to phrase it, 'instructional', not merely 'inspirational', service. But aptness to teach alone does not make a minister; nor is it his primary qualification. It is only one of a long list of requirements which Paul lays down as necessary to meet in him who aspires to this high office. And all the rest concern, not his intellectual, but his spiritual fitness. A minister must be learned, on pain of being utterly incompetent for his work. But before and above being learned, a minister must be godly. Nothing could be more fatal, however, than to set these two things over against one another. Recruiting officers do not dispute whether it is better for soldiers to have a right leg or a left leg: soldiers should have both legs. Sometimes we hear it said that ten minutes on your knees will give you a truer, deeper, more operative knowledge of God than ten hours over your books. 'What!', is the appropriate response, 'than ten hours over your books, on your knees?' Why should you turn from God when you turn to your books, or feel that you must turn from your books in order to turn to God? If learning and devotion are as antagonistic as that, then the intellectual life is in itself accursed, and there can be no question of a religious life for a student, even of theology. The mere fact that he is a student inhibits religion for him. That I am asked to speak to you on the religious life of the student of theology proceeds on the recognition of the absurdity of such antitheses. You are students of theology; and, just because you are students of theology, it is understood that you are religious men — especially religious men, to whom the cultivation of your religious life is a matter of the profoundest concern—of such concern that you will wish above all things to be warned of the dangers that may assail your religious life, and be pointed to the means by which you may strengthen and enlarge it. In your case there can be no 'either/or' here—either a student or a man of God. You must be both.

Perhaps the intimacy of the relation between the work of a theological student and his religious life will nevertheless bear some emphasizing. Of course you do not think religion and study incompatible. But it is barely possible that there may be some among you who think of them too much apart—who are inclined to set their studies off to one side, and their religious life off to the other side, and to fancy that what is given to the one is taken from the other. No mistake could be more gross. Religion does not take a man away from his work; it sends him to his work with an added quality of devotion. We sing—do we not?—

> Teach me, my God and King,
>   In all things Thee to see—
> And what I do in anything,
>   To do it as for Thee.
>
> If done t'obey Thy laws,
>   E'en servile labours shine,

> Hallowed is toil, if this the cause,
>   The meanest work divine.

It is not just the way George Herbert wrote it. He put, perhaps, a sharper point on it. He reminds us that a man may look at his work as he looks at a pane of glass—either seeing nothing but the glass, or looking straight through the glass to the wide heavens beyond. And he tells us plainly that there is nothing so mean but that the great words, 'for thy sake', can glorify it:

> A servant, with this clause,
>   Makes drudgery divine,
> Who sweeps a room as for Thy laws,
>   Makes that, and the action, fine.

But the doctrine is the same, and it is the doctrine, the fundamental doctrine, of Protestant morality, from which the whole system of Christian ethics unfolds. It is the great doctrine of 'vocation', the doctrine, to wit, that the best service we can offer to God is just to do our duty—our plain, homely duty, whatever that may chance to be.

The Middle Ages did not think so; they cut a cleft between the religious and the secular life, and counselled him who wished to be religious to turn his back on what they called 'the world', that is to say, not the wickedness that is in the world—'the world, the flesh and the devil', as we say—but the work-a-day world, that congeries of occupations which forms the daily task of men and women, who perform their duty to themselves and their fellow men. Protestantism put an end to all that. As Professor Doumergue eloquently puts it,

> Then Luther came, and, with still more consistency, Calvin, proclaiming the great idea of 'vocation', an idea and a word which are found in the languages of all the Protestant peoples— *Beruf, Calling, Vocation*—and which are lacking in the languages of the peoples of antiquity and of medieval culture. 'Vocation'—it is the call of God, addressed to every man, whoever he may be, to lay upon him a particular work, no matter what. And the calls, and therefore also the called, stand on a complete equality with one another. The burgomaster is God's burgomaster; the physician is God's physician; the merchant is God's merchant; the labourer is God's labourer. Every vocation, liberal, as we call it, or manual, the humblest and the vilest in appearance as truly as the noblest and the most glorious, is of divine right.

Talk of the divine right of kings! Here is the divine right of every workman, no one of whom needs to be ashamed, if only he is an honest and good workman.

'Only laziness', adds Professor Doumergue, 'is ignoble, and while Romanism multiplies its mendicant orders, the Reformation banishes the idle from its towns.'

Now, as students of theology your vocation is to study theology; and to study it diligently, in accordance with the apostolic injunction: 'Whatsoever ye do, do it heartily, as to the Lord.' It is precisely for this that you are students of theology; this is your 'next duty', and the neglect of duty is not a fruitful religious exercise. Dr Charles Hodge, in his delightful autobiographical notes, tells of Philip Lindsay, the most popular professor in the Princeton College of his day—a man sought by nearly every college in the central States for its presidency—that 'he told our class that we would find that one of the best preparations for death was a thorough knowledge of the Greek grammar'. 'This', comments Dr Hodge, in his quaint fashion, 'was his way of telling us that we ought to do our duty.' Certainly, every man who aspires to be a religious man must begin by doing his duty, his obvious duty, his daily task, the particular work which lies before him to do at this particular time and place. If this work happens to be studying, then his religious life depends on nothing more fundamentally than on just studying. You might as well talk of a father who neglects his parental duties, of a son who fails in all the obligations of filial piety, of an artisan who systematically skimps his work and turns in a bad job, of a workman who is nothing better than an eye-servant, being religious men as of a student who does not study being a religious man. It cannot be: you cannot build up a religious life except you begin by performing faithfully your simple, daily duties. It is not the question whether you like these duties. You may think of your studies what you please. You may consider that you are singing precisely of them when you sing of 'e'en servile labours', and of 'the meanest work'. But you must faithfully give yourselves to your studies, if you wish to be religious men. No religious character can be built up on the foundation of neglected duty.

There is certainly something wrong with the religious life of a theological student who does not study. But it does not quite follow that therefore everything is right with his religious life if he does study. It is possible to study—even to study theology—in an entirely secular spirit. I said a little while ago that what religion does is to send a man to his work with an added quality of devotion. In saying that, I meant the word 'devotion' to be taken in both its senses—in the sense of 'zealous application', and in the sense of 'a religious exercise', as the Standard Dictionary phrases the two definitions. A truly religious man will study anything which it becomes his duty to study with 'devotion' in both of these senses.

That is what his religion does for him: it makes him do his duty, do it thoroughly, do it 'in the Lord'.

But in the case of many branches of study, there is nothing in the topics studied which tends directly to feed the religious life, or to set in movement the religious emotions, or to call out specifically religious reaction. If we study them 'in the Lord', that is only because we do it 'for his sake', on the principle which makes 'sweeping a room' an act of worship. With theology it is not so. In all its branches alike, theology has as its unique end to make God known: the student of theology is brought by his daily task into the presence of God, and is kept there. Can a religious man stand in the presence of God, and not worship? It is possible, I have said, to study even theology in a purely secular spirit. But surely that is possible only for an irreligious man, or at least for an unreligious man. And here I place in your hands at once a touchstone by which you may discern your religious state, and an instrument for the quickening of your religious life. Do you prosecute your daily tasks as students of theology as 'religious exercises'? If you do not, look to yourselves: it is surely not all right with the spiritual condition of that man who can busy himself daily with divine things, with a cold and impassive heart. If you do, rejoice. But in any case, see that you do! And that you do it ever more and more abundantly.

Whatever you may have done in the past, for the future make all your theological studies 'religious exercises'. This is the great rule for a rich and wholesome religious life in a theological student. Put your heart into your studies; do not merely occupy your mind with them, but put your heart into them. They bring you daily and hourly into the very presence of God; his ways, his dealing with men, the infinite majesty of his being form their very subject-matter. Put the shoes from off your feet in this holy presence!

We are frequently told, indeed, that the great danger of the theological student lies precisely in his constant contact with divine things. They may come to seem common to him, because they are customary. As the average man breathes the air and basks in the sunshine without ever a thought that it is God in his goodness who makes his sun to rise on him, though he is evil, and sends rain to him, though he is unjust; so you may come to handle even the furniture of the sanctuary with never a thought above the gross earthly materials of which it is made. The words which tell you of God's terrible majesty or of his glorious goodness may come to be mere words to you—Hebrew and Greek words, with etymologies, and inflections, and connections in sentences. The reasonings which establish to you the mysteries of his saving activities may come to be to you mere logical paradigms, with premises and conclusions, fitly framed, no doubt, and triumphantly cogent, but with no further significance to you than their formal logical conclusiveness. God's stately stepping in his redemptive processes may become to you a mere series of facts of history, curiously interplaying to the production of social and religious conditions, and pointing mayhap to an issue which we may shrewdly conjecture; but much like other facts occurring in time and space, which may come to your notice. It is your great danger. But it is your great danger, only because it is your great privilege. Think of what your privilege is when your greatest danger is that the great things of religion may become common to you! Other men, oppressed by the hard conditions of life, sunk in the daily struggle for bread perhaps, distracted at any rate by the dreadful drag of the world upon them and the awful rush of the world's work, find it hard to get time and opportunity so much as to pause and consider whether there be such things as God, and religion, and salvation from the sin that compasses them about and holds them captive. The very atmosphere of your life is these things; you breathe them in at every pore; they surround you, encompass you, press in upon you from every side. It is all in danger of becoming common to you! God forgive you, you are in danger of becoming weary of God!

Do you know what this danger is? Or, rather, let us turn the question—are you alive to what your privileges are? Are you making full use of them? Are you, by this constant contact with divine things, growing in holiness, becoming every day more and more men of God?

If not, you are hardening! And I am here today to warn you to take seriously your theological study, not merely as a duty, done for God's sake and therefore made divine, but as a religious exercise, itself charged with religious blessing to you; as fitted by its very nature to fill all your mind and heart and soul and life with divine thoughts and feelings and aspirations and achievements. You will never prosper in your religious life in the theological seminary until your work in the theological seminary becomes itself to you a religious exercise out of which you draw every day enlargement of heart, elevation of spirit, and adoring delight in your Maker and your Saviour.

I am not counselling you, you will observe, to make your theological studies your sole religious exercises. They are religious exercises of the most rewarding kind; and your religious life will very much depend upon your treating them as such. But there are other religious exercises demanding your punctual attention which cannot be neglected without the gravest damage to your religious life. I refer particularly now to the stated formal religious meetings of the seminary. I wish to be perfectly explicit here, and very emphatic. No man can withdraw himself from the stated religious services of the community of which he is a member, without serious injury to his personal religious life. It is not without significance that the apostolic writer couples together the exhortations, 'to hold fast the confession of our hope, that it waver not', and 'to forsake not the assembling of ourselves together'. When he commands us not to forsake 'the assembling of ourselves together', he has in mind, as the term he employs shows, the stated, formal assemblages of the community, and means to lay upon the hearts and consciences of his readers their duty to the church of which they are the supports, as well as their duty to themselves. And when he adds, 'as the custom of some is', he means to put a lash into his command. We can see his lip curl as he says it.

Who are these people, who are so vastly strong, so supremely holy, that they do not need the assistance of the common worship for themselves; and who, being so strong and holy, will not give their assistance to the common worship?

Needful as common worship is, however, for men at large, the need of it for men at large is as nothing compared with its needfulness for a body of young men situated as you are. You are gathered together here for a religious purpose, in preparation for the highest religious service which can be performed by men—the guidance of others in the religious life; and shall you have everything else in common except worship? You are gathered together here, separated from your homes and all that home means; from the churches in which you have been brought up, and all that church fellowship means; from all the powerful natural influences of social religion—and shall you not yourselves form a religious community, with its own organic religious life and religious expression? I say it deliberately, that a body of young men, living apart in a community life, as you are and must be living, cannot maintain a healthy, full, rich religious life individually, unless they are giving organic expression to their religious life as a community in frequent stated diets of common worship. Nothing can take the place of this common organic worship of the community as a community, at its stated seasons, and as a regular function of the corporate life of the community. Without it you cease to be a religious community and lack that support and stay, that incitement and spur, that comes to the individual from the organic life of the community of which he forms a part.

In my own mind, I am quite clear that in an institution like this the whole body of students should come together, both morning and evening, every day, for common prayer; and should join twice on every Sabbath in formal worship. Without at least this much common worship I do not think the institution can preserve its character as a distinctively religious institution—an institution whose institutional life is primarily a religious one. And I do not think that the individual students gathered here can, with less full expression of the organic religious life of the institution, preserve the high level of religious life on which, as students of theology, they ought to live. You will observe that I am not merely exhorting you 'to go to church'. 'Going to church' is in any case good. But what I am exhorting you to do is go to your own church—to give your presence and active religious participation to every stated meeting for worship of the institution as an institution. Thus you will do your part to give to the institution an organic religious life, and you will draw out from the organic religious life of the institution a support and inspiration for your own personal religious life which you can get nowhere else, and which you can cannot afford to miss—if, that is, you have a care to your religious quickening and growth. To be an active member of a living religious body is the condition of healthy religious functioning. I trust you will not tell me that the stated religious exercises of the seminary are too numerous, or are wearying. That would only be to betray the low ebb of your own religious vitality. The feet of him whose heart is warm with religious feeling turn of themselves to the sanctuary, and carry him with joyful steps to the house of prayer. I am told that there are some students who do not find themselves in a prayerful mood in the early hours of a winter morning; and are much too tired at the close of a hard day's work to pray, and therefore do not find it profitable to attend prayers in the late afternoon: who think the preaching at the regular service on Sabbath morning dull and uninteresting, and who do not find Christ at the Sabbath afternoon conference. Such things I seem to have heard before; and yours will be an exceptional pastorate, if you do not hear something very like them, before you have been in a pastorate six months. Such things meet you every day on the street; they are the ordinary expression of the heart which is dulled or is dulling to the religious appeal. They are not hopeful symptoms among those whose life should be lived on the religious heights. No doubt, those who minister to you in spiritual things should take them to heart. And you who are ministered to must take them to heart, too. And let me tell you straight out that the preaching you find dull will no more seem dull to you if you faithfully obey the Master's precept: 'Take heed how ye hear'; that if you do not find Christ in the conference room it is because you do not take him there with you; that, if after an ordinary day's work you are too weary to unite with your fellows in closing the day with common prayer, it is because the impulse to prayer is weak in your heart. If there is no fire in the pulpit it falls to you to kindle it in the pews. No man can fail to meet with God in the sanctuary if he takes God there with him.

How easy it is to roll the blame of our cold hearts over upon the shoulders of our religious leaders! It is refreshing to observe how Luther, with his breezy good sense, dealt with complaints of lack of attractiveness in his evangelical preachers. He had not sent them out to please people, he said, and their function was not to interest or to entertain; their function was to teach the saving truth of God, and, if they did that, it was frivolous for people in danger of perishing for want of the truth to object to the vessel in which it was offered to them.

When the people of Torgau, for instance, wished to dismiss their pastors, because, they said, their voices were too weak to fill the churches, Luther simply responded, 'That's an old song: better have some difficulty in hearing the gospel than no difficulty at all in hearing what is very far from the gospel.' 'People cannot have their ministers exactly as they wish', he declares again, 'they should thank God for the pure word', and

not demand St Augustines and St Ambroses to preach it
to them. If a pastor pleases the Lord Jesus and is faithful
to him,—there is none so great and mighty but he ought
to be pleased with him, too. The point, you see, is that
men who are hungry for the truth and get it ought not
to be exigent as to the platter in which it is served to
them. And they will not be.

But why should we appeal to Luther? Have we not
the example of our Lord Jesus Christ? Are we better
than he? Surely, if ever there was one who might justly
plead that the common worship of the community had
nothing to offer him it was the Lord Jesus Christ. But
every Sabbath found him seated in his place among the
worshipping people, and there was no act of stated worship which he felt himself entitled to discard. Even in his
most exalted moods, and after his most elevating experiences, he quietly took his place with the rest of God's
people, sharing with them in the common worship of
the community. Returning from that great baptismal
scene, when the heavens themselves were rent to bear
him witness that he was well pleasing to God; from the
searching trials of the wilderness, and from that first
great tour in Galilee, prosecuted, as we are expressly
told, 'in the power of the Spirit'; he came back, as the
record tells, 'to Nazareth, where he had been brought
up, and'—so proceeds the amazing narrative—'he

entered, as his custom was, into the synagogue, on the Sabbath day'. 'As his custom was'! Jesus Christ made it his habitual practice to be found in his place on the Sabbath day at the stated place of worship to which he belonged. 'It is a reminder', as Sir William Robertson Nicoll well insists, 'of the truth which, in our fancied spirituality, we are apt to forget—that the holiest personal life can scarcely afford to dispense with stated forms of devotion, and that the regular public worship of the church, for all its local imperfections and dullness, is a divine provision for sustaining the individual soul.' 'We cannot afford to be wiser than our Lord in this matter. If anyone could have pled that his spiritual experience was so lofty that it did not require public worship, if anyone might have felt that the consecration and communion of his personal life exempted him from what ordinary mortals needed, it was Jesus. But he made no such plea. Sabbath by Sabbath even he was found in the place of worship, side by side with God's people, not for the mere sake of setting a good example, but for deeper reasons. Is it reasonable, then, that any of us should think we can safely afford to dispense with the pious custom of regular participation with the common worship of our locality?' Is it necessary for me to exhort those who would fain be like Christ, to see to it that they are imitators of him in this?

But not even with the most assiduous use of the corporate expressions of the religious life of the community have you reached the foundation stone of your piety. That is to be found, of course, in your closets, or rather in your hearts, in your private religious exercises, and in your intimate religious aspirations. You are here as theological students; and if you would be religious men, you must do your duty as theological students; you must find daily nourishment for your religious life in your theological studies, you must enter fully into the organic religious life of the community of which you form a part. But to do all this you must keep the fires of religious life burning brightly in your heart; in the inmost core of your being, you must be men of God.

Time would fail me, if I undertook to outline with any fulness the method of the devout life. Every soul seeking God honestly and earnestly finds him, and, in finding him, finds the way to him. One hint I may give you, particularly adapted to you as students for the ministry: Keep always before your mind the greatness of your calling, that is to say, these two things: the immensity of the task before you, the infinitude of the resources at your disposal.

I think it has not been idly said, that if we face the tremendous difficulty of the work before us, it will certainly throw us back upon our knees; and if we worthily gauge the power of the gospel committed to us, that will certainly keep us on our knees. I am led to single out this particular consideration, because it seems to me that we have fallen upon an age in which we very greatly need to recall ourselves to the seriousness of life and its issues, and to the seriousness of our calling as ministers to life. Sir Oliver Lodge informs us that 'men of culture are not bothering', nowadays, 'about their sin, much less about their punishment', and Dr Johnston Ross preaches us a much needed homily from that text on the 'light-heartedness of the modern religious quest'. In a time like this, it is perhaps not strange that careful observers of the life of our theological seminaries tell us that the most noticeable thing about it is a certain falling off from the intense seriousness of outlook by which students of theology were formerly characterized. Let us hope it is not true. If it were true, it would be a great evil; so far as it is true, it is a great evil. I would call you back to this seriousness of outlook, and bid you cultivate it, if you would be men of God now, and ministers who need not be ashamed hereafter. Think of the greatness of the minister's calling; the greatness of the issues which hang on your worthiness or your unworthiness for its high functions; and determine once for all that with God's help you will be worthy. 'God had but one Son', says Thomas Goodwin, 'and he made him a minister.' 'None but he who made the world', says John Newton, 'can make a minister'—that is, a minister who is worthy. You can, of course, be a minister of a sort, and not be Godmade.

You can go through the motions of the work, and I shall not say that your work will be in vain—for God is good and who knows by what instruments he may work his will of good for men? Helen Jackson pictures far too common an experience when she paints the despair of one whose sowing, though not unfruitful for others, bears no harvest in his own soul.

> O teacher, then I said, thy years,
> Are they not joy? each word that issueth
> From out thy lips, doth it return to bless
> Thine own heart manyfold?

Listen to the response:

> I starve with hunger treading out their corn,
> I die of travail while their souls are born.

She does not mean it in quite the evil part in which I am reading it. But what does Paul mean when he utters that terrible warning: 'Lest when I have preached to others, I myself should be a castaway?' And there is an even more dreadful contingency. It is our Saviour himself who tells us that it is possible to compass sea and land to make one proselyte, and when we have made him to make him twofold more a child of hell than we are ourselves. And will we not be in awful peril of making our proselytes children of hell if we are not ourselves children of heaven? Even physical waters will not rise above their source: the spiritual floods are even less tractable to our commands.

There is no mistake more terrible than to suppose that activity in Christian work can take the place of depth of Christian affections. This is the reason why many good men are shaking their heads a little today over a tendency which they fancy they see increasing among our younger Christian workers to restless activity at the apparent expense of depth of spiritual culture. Activity, of course, is good: surely in the cause of the Lord we should run and not be weary. But not when it is substituted for inner religious strength. We cannot get along without our Marthas. But what shall we do when, through all the length and breadth of the land, we shall search in vain for a Mary? Of course the Marys will be as little admired by the Marthas today as of yore. 'Lord', cried Martha, 'dost thou not care that my sister hath left me to serve alone?' And from that time to this the cry has continually gone up against the Marys that they waste the precious ointment which might have been given to the poor, when they pour it out to God, and are idle when they sit at the Master's feet.

A minister, high in the esteem of the churches, is even quoted as declaring—not confessing, mind you, but publishing abroad as something in which he gloried— that he has long since ceased to pray: he works. 'Work and pray' is no longer, it seems, to be the motto of at least ministerial life. It is to be all work and no praying; the only prayer that is prevailing, we are told, with the same cynicism with which we are told that God is on the side of the largest battalions—is just work. You will say this is an extreme case. Thank God, it is. But in the tendencies of our modern life, which all make for ceaseless—I had almost said thoughtless, meaningless— activity, have a care that it does not become your case; or that your case—even now—may not have at least some resemblance to it. Do you pray? How much do you pray? How much do you love to pray? What place in your life does the 'still hour', alone with God, take?

I am sure that if you once get a true glimpse of what the ministry of the cross is, for which you are preparing, and of what you, as men preparing for this ministry, should be, you will pray, 'Lord, who is sufficient for these things', your heart will cry; and your whole soul will be wrung with the petition: 'Lord, make me sufficient for these things.' Old Cotton Mather wrote a great little book once, to serve as a guide to students for the ministry. The not very happy title which he gave it is

Manductio ad Ministerium. But by a stroke of genius he added a sub-title which is more significant. And this is the sub-title he added: *The angels preparing to sound the trumpets.* That is what Cotton Mather calls you, students for the ministry: *the angels, preparing to sound the trumpets!* Take the name to yourselves, and live up to it. Give your days and nights to living up to it! And then, perhaps, when you come to sound the trumpets the note will be pure and clear and strong, and perchance may pierce even to the grave and wake the dead.

Let's Study Series

Series Editor – Sinclair B. Ferguson

'The whole unfolding Let's Study series is a must for every Christian home that is serious about getting to know the Word.' — COVENANTER WITNESS

Let's Study Matthew by Mark Ross
Let's Study Mark by Sinclair B. Ferguson
Let's Study Luke by Douglas Milne
Let's Study John by Mark Johnston
Let's Study Acts by Denis E. Johnson
Let's Study 1 Corinthians by Derek Jackman
Let's Study 2 Corinthians by Derek Prime
Let's Study Galatians by Derek Thomas
Let's Study Ephesians by Sinclair B. Ferguson
Let's Study Philippians by Sinclair B. Ferguson
Let's Study Colossians & Philemon by Mark Johnston
Let's Study 1 & 2 Thessalonians by Andrew W. Young
Let's Study 1 Timothy by W. John Cook
Let's Study Hebrews by Hywel R. Jones
Let's Study 1 Peter by William Harrell
Let's Study 2 Peter & Jude by Mark Johnston
Let's Study the Letters of John by Ian Hamilton
Let's Study Revelation by Derek Thomas

Large format paperback.

Each volume includes a 13-week study guide.

William Hendriksen's New Testament Commentaries

'I know of no finer commentaries in the English language.' – Edwin Palmer

Matthew, 1024pp.
Mark, 712pp.
Luke, 1124pp.
John, 768pp.
Romans, 548pp.
Galatians and Ephesians, 568pp.
Philippians, Colossians and Philemon, 480pp.
1 & 2 Thessalonians, 1 & 2 Timothy, and Titus, 632pp.

All published in quality cloth-bound volumes.
Available from the Banner of Truth Trust website:
www.banneroftruth.org

'*The New Testament Commentary* is admirably clear, both in analysis and exegesis. While dealing realistically with interpretative problems when they arise, its primary interest lies in the positive elucidation of the text. Dr Hendriksen succeeds in satisfying the demands both of the biblical student and the preacher in search of homiletical material – a combination all too rare today.'

– A. Skevington Wood, *The Life of Faith*